The Family Album

★
★　　★
★　★　★　★　★
★　　★
★

The Family Album

Edited by
ARTHUR AND NANCY DeMOSS

Associate Editor
JOSEPH V. GORMAN

Published by
A. J. HOLMAN COMPANY
Division of J. B. Lippincott Company
Philadelphia and New York

ISBN 0-87981-066-1

COPYRIGHT MCMLXXVI BY

THE FAMILY ALBUM

VALLEY FORGE, PENNSYLVANIA

ALL RIGHTS RESERVED

LIBRARY OF CONGRESS CATALOG CARD NUMBER 66-21900

PRINTED IN THE UNITED STATES OF AMERICA

ACKNOWLEDGMENTS

Grateful acknowledgment is hereby expressed to all those who have contributed to this book. Any inadvertent omissions of credit will be gladly corrected in future editions.

ABINGDON PRESS for "I'm burdened down, Lord" from *Too Busy Not To Pray*, by Jo Carr and Imogene Sorley. Copyright © 1966 by Abingdon Press. Used by permission of Abingdon Press.

AMERICAN BAPTIST BOARD OF EDUCATION AND PUBLICATION for material from *The Secret Place* by Ruth H. Short, Donald B. Taylor and Robert A. Moore. Used by permission of the American Baptist Board of Education and Publication.

AUGSBURG PUBLISHING HOUSE for "Growing in Prayer" from *Praise God For This New Day* by Catherine Brandt, Copyright © 1975 Augsburg Publishing House. Used by permission.

CHICAGO TRIBUNE—NEW YORK NEWS SYNDICATE, INC. for "You Can't Change the Color" by Billy Graham.

CHRISTIAN LIVING for "What's a Table For?" by Doris Longacre. Used by permission from *Christian Living*, Copyright © 1974 by Mennonite Publishing House, Scottsdale, PA.

CHRISTIANITY TODAY for "O God, Our Father, Ruler of All Nations" by Mrs. Moncrief Jordan. Copyright © 1975 by *Christianity Today*. Also, for "Out of This Night" by M. Whitcomb Hess. Copyright © 1975 by *Christianity Today*. Used by permission.

COLLINS-KNOWLTON-WING, INC. for material from *Hill Country Harvest* by Hal Borland. Reprinted by permission of Collins-Knowlton-Wing, Inc. Copyright © 1967 by Hal Borland.

DECISION for "The Business" from *Decision*, Copyright © 1971 by Billy Graham Evang. Assn.

ACKNOWLEDGMENTS continued on page 176

Contents

Editors' Foreword

Anniversaries seem to have taken on a new significance in this Bicentennial year. Thus we cannot help noting that as America begins its third century, the Family Album begins its second decade of publication with this eleventh edition.

During those first ten years one of our greatest joys each year has been to see each new volume come from the printers. Suddenly in printed form and in brilliant color we saw all of our efforts during the past twelve months come together. Even as we had asked for God's direction as we selected the material, so then we asked for His blessing in the hearts and lives of each of the readers.

We have done the same this year, and send this volume forth with our prayers that some new appreciation of God's great goodness to us all will emerge as you read the words and enjoy the pictures that make up this eleventh edition.

Now as we begin work on the next Family Album, we will, as always, appreciate your letters, comments and suggestions—for which we offer our thanks in advance.

Sincerely,

Arthur and Nancy DeMoss
Valley Forge, Pennsylvania

The Family Album

the GREAT BOOKS ARE those that GROW with man.

JEAN ROSTAND

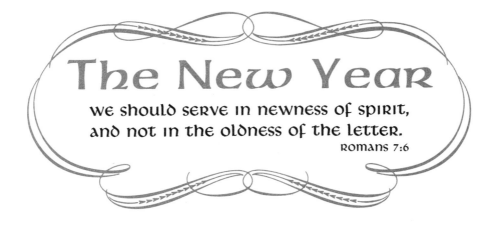

The New Year

we should serve in newness of spirit,
and not in the oldness of the letter.

ROMANS 7:6

This Will Be A Great Year

I believe in the beauty, the possibilities and the promises of this year. Seeds that are now sleeping in the bosom of the earth will awaken, break through the surface of the soil and become sturdy plants, beautiful flowers and nourishing food. Trees that are now barren of leaves will burst forth again in the spring to provide assurance, shade and fruit as they have since time began.

Tiny bodies that are now growing and developing inside their mothers will become healthy babies who will be loved, cared for and nurtured. Caterpillars will become butterflies; dreams will become realities. God's sun will rise each morning. His rain will fall. His mountains will stand. His rainbows will give radiant promise of even greater tomorrows.

God's truth will be recognized. His love will be expressed. His joy will be experienced. His presence will be felt.

Ideas that now lie dormant in the minds of man will find complete expression this year. Poems and books that are now but embryos will mature into classics of wisdom and inspiration. Man's prayers will be heard and answered. Friendships will be formed and strengthened. Difficulties will be met and mastered. Challenges will be faced and conquered. Victories will be achieved and celebrated.

I confidently expect this to be a great year, because I constantly will be looking for the best. *William Arthur Ward*

I Pack My Trunk

What shall I pack up to carry
 From the old year to the new?
I'll leave out the frets that harry,
 Thoughts unjust and doubts untrue.

Angry words—ah, how I rue them!
 Selfish deeds and choices blind;
Any one is welcome to them!
 I shall leave them all behind.

But I'll pack the sweet remembrance
 Of dear friendship's least delight;
All my jokes—I'll carry them hence;
 All my store of fancies bright:

My contentment—would 'twere greater!
 All the courage I possess;
All my trust—there's not much weight there!
 All my faith, or more or less.

And I'll pack my choicest treasures:
 Smiles I've seen and praises heard,
Memories of unselfish pleasures,
 Cheery looks, the kindly word.

Amos R. Wells

New Year

And now I have my New Year book to fill;
No word yet penned in it, nor any blot
Upon the clean white sheets, the pages still
Uncut, though dated day by day. Just what
They will record, God only can foretell—
And, after all, perhaps it is as well.

Ethel Romig Fuller

Thin Ice

The temperature had hovered between freezing and zero for almost a week. When I got home from work, I glanced at the frozen Rocky River, just a few feet from our door—and it looked inviting.

"What about having some friends over for skating tonight?" I asked my wife Sylva. Whenever the ice was good, we liked to flood-light the area behind our house and play skating music on the hi-fi. Afterward skaters would come upstairs for cookies and coffee before a roaring fire in our living room. But this time Sylva said no. She had been working since seven a.m., so she was very tired.

The sun was still shining and I figured there would be a good half hour before dark for me to skate. Down the stairs I went and put on my skates on the dock under our house. The ice tested very strong, the temperature was 22 degrees and there was no wind—a great combination. It was exhilarating. At a smooth clip I traveled across the lagoon in back of our house and suddenly felt so invigorated that I decided to skate on—to the river, up the west channel and around the island on which the Cleveland Yachting Club is located. The club was closed and it looked like a ghost town of dry-docked boats.

"Great skating!" I shouted happily to a woman skating with some children, the only people around. I shot ahead, under the little bridge that connected the island to the far bank, on and on until I headed once more into the river, clipping along 100 feet from shore, when . . .

Oh, oh—a patch of soft ice. Slush. I thought I could coast through it, but I slowed down. I stroked with my right foot; the ice gave way under it. I tried to stroke with the other, but *it* broke through. I was in trouble. Bad trouble.

Immediately I knew why. It was because of the big bridge high above me. For days the city had been spreading salt on it to melt the snow on the roadbed. The salt had filtered down to the river, softening the wide path of ice I had skated into. Now I found myself sinking through the ice, then suddenly plunging up to my neck in freezing water.

I did not panic. I hollered; I pounded away at the mushy ice in an attempt to reach ice firm enough to support me. I know I had to do something fast, for I had read somewhere that a person can survive only three minutes in freezing water. I was aware, too, of an unusual fact about myself—that I am incapable of floating. I'm so thin, more bones than flesh, that I have what is called negative buoyancy—when I'm not moving my arms or legs in water, I sink.

I tried to work myself toward firmer ice by breaking off small pieces along the edge. But it was taking too much time. This way I'd freeze to death before I'd ever get out. The bridge above me was humming with rush-hour traffic, yet I knew, because of the railing and the angle, that no one in a passing car could see me. I simply had to think of another way to get myself out of the water.

I swim regularly and it was not unusual for me to swim the length of the "Y" pool underwater. I looked at the shore 100 feet away and realized that if I could swim that distance under the ice, I could break through at the shore. I took one last look around to see if anyone was in sight. No one. "And if I don't make it," I said to myself, "no one except God will ever know what happened."

There in the water, about to dive under the ice, thinking of God, I felt ashamed before Him. "I'm sorry," I prayed to Him. "I'm sorry I've been so careless with Your precious gift of life. I want to live, God. I want desperately to live, but I'll accept Your will."

I wasn't asking Him for help or for my life, yet now He was present; I could feel His closeness as I prepared myself for the plunge.

Don't do it! came the feeling. I was mystified. I had set my mind on the plan. *Don't do it!* came the feeling again.

My mind told me one thing, but His presence told me another. I had to decide now. I gave myself over to that inner command.

It was a matter of minutes, maybe two, when I saw the police car on the yachting-club island and nearby, across the stretch of obviously treacherous ice, I saw a policeman standing in the dusk, looking at me. "Throw me a rope!" I yelled. He disappeared. "Hurry," I said to myself frantically. "Hurry!" Could he know how little time I had left?

I heard voices. "We're going to throw you a rope."

Throw it now! I thought to myself. I could feel the paralysis setting in. It came fast. At first I couldn't move my legs. My arms stiffened. No longer now was I thinking about ropes. I was thinking about . . . boyhood vacations on Mackinac Island . . . Sylva and I on a flying honeymoon . . . sailing on a moonlit night . . .

I saw my hands slip away from the surface of the ice. Yet I was experiencing a peace that was serene and actually pleasant. I felt my head go under the water. I felt icy water entering my mouth. I was sinking, but now I could move neither arms nor legs.

And then, suddenly, mysteriously, the power was there. I *could* move my arms. I pushed them down in the water. My head came up. I breathed again. And there in front of me was an orange life preserver. The last thing I remember was reaching for it.

My next awareness was opening my eyes and seeing the doctor peering into my face. He said, "There's someone here I'm sure you want to see." It was Sylva.

"How did I get here?" I asked, bewildered. Her answer was a litany of many miracles.

A bus was crossing the bridge at the precise moment I fell through the ice. The driver, sitting high up, saw me and radioed his dis-

Continued on page 12

Continued from page 11

patcher, who called the police. A girl happened to be walking along our river-front road on her way to a baby-sitting job. She heard my cries for help and rushed to our neighbor's house. The neighbor stepped outside, saw me in the river, and also called the police.

A policeman came, then went to his car to radio for extra help, while I held on to the orange life preserver that had been thrown to me. My rescuers were able to walk about halfway out on the ice before it started to crack, and a rope was thrown, which they say I grabbed, but let slip when they started to pull on it.

By then, a crowd had gathered on the island. Three times my head went under the water, each time the crowd gasping, shouting that I was gone, and three times my head came back up, spouting water. Finally, a dinghy was found and one of the policemen rushed it to the spot where I was appearing and disappearing. I was submerged, completely out of sight before he could get to me, but he reached his arm down over the dinghy into the water and, miraculously, connected with the collar of my jacket. The dinghy nearly capsized as he tried to drag me into it, but he hung on to me and we were pulled to safety. Oxygen kept me alive during the rush to the hospital.

Later, I figured that I was in the freezing water a minimum of 12 minutes. I was unconscious for three hours. The doctor in the emergency room at the hospital said he never saw a person alive with a pH blood factor as low as mine—six. I was shivering from cold when I came to, calling for blankets. I spent the one night in the intensive-care unit and, to the doctors' amazement, the patient who was in critical condition on arrival was permitted to return home the next day. Two months later my heart was back to normal, and eight months later the nerves in my arms and legs had regenerated.

It took about a week for me to believe fully that I wasn't just dreaming and was really living. Since then, life for me has taken on a new meaning. I am more appreciative of being alive. I feel very grateful to God for sparing my life and to the five people who had a major part in my rescue. Since then, too, a lot of questions have been answered for me.

Where did the message come from that stopped me from my rash plan to swim under the ice?

When my body was paralyzed, where did the power come from that let my arms move again?

When I was unconscious under the water, why didn't the current sweep me downstream?

I know the answers to those questions now, for I've learned that God is always listening. He hears our prayers. When it is within His plan to answer them, He can work miracles. He did for me.

William G. Benkelman

Storm's End

The snowflakes clung upon each pane
Like baby hands of porcelain,
Until the wind with awesome force
Eddied the snow in a whirlpool course,
Amassing huge drifts to pile sill-high
A barricade which hid the sky.
When silence shawled the whitened earth,
Within that hush one sensed re-birth.

Dorothy E. Zimmerman

The Pathway of Winter

Walk a winter path,
    and prepare for a journey to paradise.
Tread a winter carpet
    of golden leaves
Strewn on grassy hillsides
    or a green forest floor,
And drift back through
    all the years of youth and memory
To recapture again, in the
    whispering crinkle of each new leaf,
The magic spell of memories
    woven from countless other walks
Along the byways of the season,
    Fragrant with the earth's
    own spicy perfume
Beneath slanting sunlight
    and cold blue skies.

Jerry Lipman

Winter Haikus

White confetti falls
softly from the winter sky
covering the lawn.

The trees are ice-decked;
they crack in the winter wind
and bend at its will.

Through the snow-filled air
a lone bird flies to a branch,
wary of the storm.

I toss him a crumb.
Cautiously he eyes the treat,
then swoops and feeds.

Could we not be friends?
I would give you bread and seeds;
you give me courage.

Jean Conder Soule

Starting A New Year

Faith, hope, and love are the expressions of this new year. God's care is very evident in life and resources. I think God's love is like the snow. It seeks so tenderly to mantle all who need His care and comes so silently.

Many of our blessings come to us without money and without price. Many of them are free ones by nature—the air, the sunshine, and the beauty of the countryside. I am filled with wonder at the many varieties of flowers and animals, and their purpose in our world.

When you are discouraged, look into the starry night when all is clear. We have so many opportunities, almost endless. Books have been written about the glories and beauty of all things in the out-of-doors. We cannot explain the reason for all endless creation, a wonderful world. When we are ill, we think of the great blessings of health; not until we are deprived of many of our blessings do we realize their worth.

So with our new year, if we do what's right, whatever comes or goes, I know we'll weather the storms. All of us have many things for which to be thankful. Thank God we face another year to live and love.

Ann L. Bangham

Let's Read It Together

the children's corner

✿✿✿✿✿✿✿✿✿✿✿✿✿✿✿✿✿✿✿✿✿✿✿✿✿✿✿✿✿✿

New Year's Resolutions

It was New Year's Day. Gathered around the dining room table were the four Barton children. Clara was twelve years old, Jack was ten, Ben was nine, and Dolly was seven. Each of them had a pen and a piece of paper on which to write their New Year's resolutions.

"I have two," Clara said. "Want to hear them?"

"Yes," said Jack and Ben and Dolly all together.

Just then Mother called from the kitchen. "Clara, have you taken care of the canary?"

"Not yet," Clara replied. "I'm busy right now."

"I'll take care of Tweetie for you," said Ben.

And so Ben cleaned Tweetie's cage, filled the seed cup, and put in fresh water. Then he went back to the table. He had just seated himself when Mother called again.

"Jack, the kitchen wastebasket is overflowing, and I suppose the others are too. Will you please empty them?"

Jack frowned. "In a little while."

"I'll do it," Ben offered.

Ben emptied all the wastebaskets, and carried out the newspapers. Then he came back, and picked up his pen. Grandmother called, "Dolly, you promised to help me sort my buttons. I'm waiting."

"In a minute," Dolly called back. "I'm busy now."

"I'll go," Ben said cheerfully.

When Ben came back, Grandfather, sitting in a rocking chair by the window, asked, "Ben, will you please get a cushion for my back?"

"Sure," Ben said. "And here's the new magazine."

Grandfather smiled. "Thanks, Ben. You're a thoughtful boy."

When Ben went back to the table, Clara and Jack had each filled one sheet of paper. As he sat down, Jack said, "I'm finished."

"What did you write?" Ben asked.

Jack began to read: "I resolve first, to be on time for school; second, to put away my clothes; third, to keep my half of our room straight; fourth, to be more kind, helpful and thoughtful; fifth, to . . ."

Clara interrupted him. "That's enough of yours. Some of them sound like mine. I have fourteen resolutions."

"I have fifteen," Jack said triumphantly.

"And I have five," said Dolly.

Continued on page 16

Continued from page 15

Clara leaned over to look at Ben's paper. "You haven't written a thing. Aren't you going to make any New Year's resolutions?"

Grandfather lowered his magazine and looked at the children over the top of his glasses. "Ben doesn't need to make resolutions about being helpful," he said. "While you were writing on paper what you were *going* to do, Ben was *doing* it—all the jobs you were asked to do and more besides."

Clara, Jack, and Dolly looked at each other, and each of them looked ashamed.

"Oh, that's all right," said Ben, as he began to write. "I don't mind. I like to help."

"No, it isn't all right!" Jack exclaimed. He tore up his paper and reached for a clean sheet. "I guess we let Ben do more than his share all the time just because he's a good guy."

Jack wrote this sentence and read it to the others: "I resolve to do my own jobs and stop letting Ben do them. Signed, Jack Barton."

Clara reached for the paper. "I'll sign it, too," she said.

"So will I," Dolly agreed.

"What are you writing, Ben?" Clara wanted to know.

Ben pushed his paper across to her. Clara read aloud, "I resolf to lern to spel this yere." She showed the paper to Jack.

"Whoopee!" said Jack. "It's about time. Let's all go out and sweep the porches and walks for Ben while he looks for his spelling book so he can get a head start on his New Year's resolution."

"Right!" Clara agreed. "And we'll help you with your spelling, Ben."

Nina Walter

Winter Magic

Our street was changed by magic
Last night to fairyland.
Where houses stood at twilight,
This morning castles stand.
Freezing raindrops coated
Each bush and blade of grass.
They changed the oaks to crystal,
Our fence to woven glass.
Each castle roof is silver
With fringe along its eaves—
A sparkling, lovely picture
That only winter leaves.

Rose Andrews

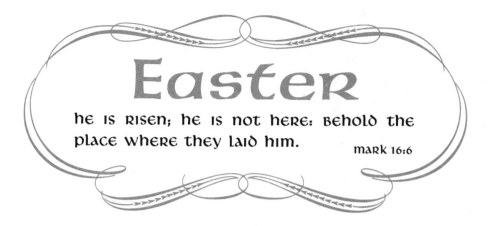

Easter

he is risen; he is not here: behold the place where they laid him.

MARK 16:6

Out Of This Night

To the world's end
Through time and tide
Jesus our Lord
Is crucified

And by His passion
And His pain
He draws all men
To Him again. . . .

(O great the grace
That buoys me up
So even I
May share His Cup!)

Still through
The darkest deeps of sin
Love seeks His own:
He calls us in

Out of this night
Of dust's despair;
And through
The angel-ambient air

Past cherubim
And seraphim
The Lord of Life
Lifts us with Him.

M. Whitcomb Hess

The Last Supper

When twilight fell in Bethany,
And shadows deepened into gloom,
Came Jesus with the twelve and sat
At supper in the upper room.

A solemn hush fell over them . . .
And in the golden candlelight
His voice was sad and choked with tears,
Knowing His hour was near that night.

"This little while I am with you,"
He said to them *"but where I go,*
I shall prepare a place for you,
That ye may be with Me also".

When He had spoken, Jesus gave
A prayer of thanks and broke the bread.
"This is my body given for you . . .
Take ye of it and eat", He said.

He took the wine cup, offering thanks,
And gave it to them lovingly:
"This is my blood, shed for your sins . . .
Drink in remembrance of Me".

They would remember all their lives
The poignant beauty in His face,
And treasure, too, the blessed words
He spoke there in that quiet place.

William Arnette Wofford

Christ In Gethsemane

Alone upon Mount Olivet,
He knelt in dark Gethsemane.
The moonlight showed His anguished face
Beneath an ancient olive tree.

Withdrawn from loved ones down the path,
The Saviour prayed in great distress,
A solitary figure spent
In agonizing loneliness.

"Oh, my Father, if it is Thy will,
Remove this dreaded cup from Me!
Not as I will, but as Thou wilt!"
He cried in His extremity.

The chill night wind sighed mournfully;
Slowly the moon began to dim;
The olive leaves in sorrow, too,
Leaned gently down to comfort Him.

His sweat was like great drops of blood
That midnight hour, kneeling there,
Until an angel sent from God
Appeared to strengthen Him in prayer.

William Arnette Wofford

Easter

There's just something in its message,
That's unrivaled for all time,
This blessed Easter message,
So rapturous and Divine—
Telling us "The Christ" of Easter
Holds within His nail-scarred hand,
All power to lift the weakest,
And break sin's deadly bands.
Yes, there's something in its message
Since that first glad Easter dawn,
For a world distraught and sinful—
It offers healing balm.
There's bright promise for tomorrow,
With life Eternal in that Day;
Through "Christ The Risen Conqueror",
Who rolled the stone away!

Helen R. Donaldson

The Easter Dress

Marly was sick of hearing about Diane's dress.

"It's got those new kind of swirly sleeves. I didn't know if I could get them set in right, but they really turned out nice! And the trim—wait till you see it, Marly. It's exactly right. Mother says I may have to sew it on by hand. But that shouldn't take too—Marly, are you listening? What's the matter? You aren't jealous, are you?"

Marly kept her eyes on the sidewalk. "Don't be silly. I just happen to have more to think about than clothes."

When they reached Diane's house, she said, "You're coming in to see it, aren't you, Marly?"

"No."

"You *are* jealous."

Marly didn't enjoy the feeling of being out of sorts, so she changed the subject. "I'll be a goner if I don't finish my geometry." But she didn't even think about her math as she walked home alone.

Two weeks ago, after her dad had written the check for Rick's third-term tuition, he asked them all to go easy on the Easter finery. She had accepted the fact that she was to have new Easter shoes, but that was all—period. When she found that Diane had gotten much the same ultimatum because her sister was getting married in May, she'd suggested they stay away from downtown and not even look at the spring things. Their agreement had worked until last week. Then Diane had said, "Guess what? I'm having a new dress for Easter, after all."

"How'd you manage that?" Marly asked.

For some reason, Diane was unable to meet her eyes. "I—uh—had some stuff that didn't fit, so I sold it and used the money for fabric."

"That's nice," Marly forced herself to say. "I may get one too." It was a lie, and Marly cringed each time she remembered.

"You're not making it, so how are you getting yours?"

Marly had lowered her voice mysteriously. "I have ways, my dear."

But the "ways" she'd had in mind hadn't worked. No amount of begging had been enough to convince her parents that she was positively destitute and would celebrate Easter in sackcloth if they didn't relent and buy her a dress. And no one had called her to baby-sit.

When Marly got home, she didn't do her geometry after all. She dreamed of being able to earn money for a dress. But since Easter was less than a week away, the plan was useless. But the next day she decided to look for an inexpensive purse to match her new Easter shoes.

Finding a purse was not as easy as Marly had expected. Prices were high in the department stores, so she decided to look in the cut-rate places. She was making her way across the street when she looked up and saw a dress in the Thrift Shop window.

It was exactly right, and it looked like her size. She started to go on by. The dress couldn't possibly be new—not in a shop that specialized in cleaning, pressing and reselling used clothing to those who could afford no better. She stopped. Who would know the difference?

An old-fashioned bell tinkled as Marly let herself into the shop. A scurrying little woman appeared from between the limp drapes that separated the two rooms. "May I help you, Dearie?" she wheezed.

Marly pointed. "That dress in the window—what size is it?"

The woman located the tag. "Seven petite. Looks like a perfect fit."

Her exact size! "How much?"

The clerk adjusted her glasses and looked again. "Five dollars, Dearie. No, it's Easter. You can have it for four."

Four she had, but not much more. "May I see it, please?"

When the dress was on the counter, Marly examined it with care. It was like new, and the label told her it was of exceptional quality. The fit was not only perfect, but the dress looked as expensive as its original price tag had probably read. "I'll take it," she said.

On the way home, she made up her mind. She would tell no more lies, but she would avoid telling Diane the source of her purchase.

The next morning as they walked to school, Marly said as casually as possible, "Well, I got my dress for Easter."

"Really! Oh, I'm glad! What color is it?" Diane was asking.

"Green."

There was a noticeable silence. Then Diane said in a choked little voice, "Pink and green. We should look nice together."

Why she's jealous now! Marly thought. She couldn't resist a dig. "The lines are really good. You can tell it came from a good shop."

"Where'd you get the money for your dress?"

Marly felt uncomfortable. "Savings from my allowance—earned the rest."

"Monday you had only three dollars."

"Look," Marly said. "Did I put you through the third degree about your old dress?" Diane colored and said no more.

That night Pastor Ellis called her. "I goofed," he said. "I was supposed to get someone to pass out programs at the Community Good Friday service tomorrow, and I completely forgot until my wife just now reminded me. Would you and one of the other girls help?"

"I'll ask Diane," Marly told him.

Diane agreed so they talked about what to wear.

"Let's wear our new Easter dresses," Marly suggested, and Diane agreed.

Marly had asked her mother to drive them to the large church downtown where the Good Friday service was to be held.

Continued on page 24

Continued from page 23

As Marly slid to the middle of the front seat to make room for Diane, she said, "Oooo—I like your dress."

Diane slammed the door and turned to look at Marly's. Her eyes widened. "I—I—yours is pretty too," she stammered.

Still jealous. Marly changed the subject, and they talked of other things the rest of the way to the church.

For a few minutes they were busy with the programs as people from all over the city made their way to the service.

As she took part in the congregational singing and listened to the brief sermon, Marly soberly asked herself the question that was printed across the front of the program—"What is Calvary to you?" At the end of the service, a group of college drama students presented scenes from around the cross.

A curtain had been drawn at the back of the platform revealing a dark scene with three crosses. In the foreground were Mary Magdalene, the weeping mother, and all of the others mentioned in the Bible. But it was the scene beneath the center cross that caught Marly's attention. Several Roman soldiers were cursing and arguing over the meager pile of garments that had been taken from Jesus.

Marly blinked back tears. "Forgive me, Jesus," she whispered.

Afterward, she said to Diane. "Those soldiers—weren't they real?"

There were tears on Diane's cheeks too. She nodded. "Yes, I—"

Marly interrupted. She had to speak before she lost her courage. "I lied to you. My dress isn't new. I bought it at the Thrift Shop."

"That's my fault. I'm the one who should apologize."

"Don't be silly. Like you said, I was jealous—"

"Marly, you don't understand. You see, my cousin sent me this box of things. She'd always been bigger than I, only now she isn't, so I sold the things to get money for fabric."

"I'd say that was pretty smart."

Diane shook her head. "Not really. Not when you know the prettiest dress of all would fit your best friend. Oh, Marly, I should have given it to you in the first place. There Jesus was, dying, and all the soldiers could think about was to fuss over clothes!"

Marly nodded. "I know. I kept thinking about that too. Easter Sunday should be a time for rejoicing—but not over who has the newest outfit. We ought to punish ourselves by wearing our oldest dresses," she said impulsively.

Diane pondered for a moment. "If we go in our new ones, perhaps it will remind us of the new way we—I, at least, intend to act."

"Me, too," Marly said. "You know, the whole thing—I mean about the dresses—is really funny when you think about it." They laughed together, and each knew the other was still her best friend.

C. Ellen Watts

Landscapes

Did you ever get up early,
Take a stroll out in the yard,
See the wet-topped blue grass shimmer,
Dressed to praise and thank the Lord?

Crystal carpet, diamond thickness,
Fields a-glimmer in the sun,
Coming through the night of darkness,
Joyous over victory won.

Here and there in multi-color,
Red and yellow, blue and green,
Dancing stones on blades so glassy,
Precious irridescent gleams.

In this sparkling jewel setting,
As you sit and meditate,
Couldn't you just stay forever
There at Heaven's open gate?

Bid all others come together,
Unify in one great whole,
Enter in, enjoy forever
Many landscapes of the soul.

Lucy L. Beemer

Untamed Gardens

Wild mustard splashes seas of gold
    in fields and on hillside.
These gardens give us joy and leave
    us gratified.
The spring has many costly gifts
    to generously bestow.
We do not toil to gain these joys
    for we reap where we do not sow.

Sophie Wormeer

golden nugget

In this fresh evening each blade and leaf looks as if it had been dipped in an icy liquid greenness. Let eyes that ache come here and look. . . .

Henry David Thoreau

Promises Of Easter

The woods are bare
And grim and bleak,
The trees stand gaunt and gray
Like soldiers armed with bayonets
To keep bright Spring away.
But pastel beauty, bravely lent,
Betrays the lovely hyacinth.

The leaves rest sodden, brown and deep;
Life seems entombed and fast asleep.
The rain in little puddles lies;
The sullen clouds hang low,
But here beneath the rain-washed skies
I watch the violets grow.

The grass seems lifeless, brown and sere,
Yet faintest signs of green appear,
And, though it is a bitter day,
Two frisky woods squirrels romp and play;
And there above the wakening sod
Three sweet-faced crocuses bravely nod.

The naked maples spread their arms
To sunless skies of gray;
The fields lie empty in the mist,

golden verse

Exclamation points of rain
Falling on the window pane,
Punctuation marks from God
To give expression to the sod.

Dorothy M. Cahoon

And snow's not far away;
But there beyond the grasses long,
I hear a cheerful robin's song.

The sky is overcast and low,
While gusty March winds rave and blow;
But there to every passer-by
The jaunty tulip flirts an eye;
Anon on every grassy hill
Will dance the graceful daffodil.

It's not too late for hail and sleet;
The rain against the windows beat.
New baby lambs crouch in the fold
For warmth and shelter from the cold.
Nipped by the wind, in mild surprise,
Wee snowdrops raise their startled eyes.

The earth beneath unsmiling lies,
Unpromising and cold;
The bearded shrubbery sadly bends
To March's chilling breath and sighs,
"Is there no life? Are all things dead?"
. . . But no, beyond the iris bed
Shy rhubarb lifts her curly head.

Ruby A. Jones

Garden In The Rain

Sweet, wet smell of earthy things,
Butterflies with folded wings,
Steady dripping, same refrain,
That's a garden in the rain.

Pale-faced pansies drooping low,
Chickens scurrying to and fro,
Gardener hobbling with his cane
Through a garden wet with rain.

Golden sunflowers reaching high
Search for sun in the leaden sky,
Snow-white lilies still remain
Fair and fragrant in the rain.

Nodding bluebells, small and sweet,
Grasses at their tender feet,
Tall, proud roses, daisies plain—
I *love* a garden in the rain.

Dorothy R. Howard

April Smiled At Me!

I had waited past the winter
For the sound of laughing creeks,
Dreaming of the fragrant woodlands
Wherein God in Nature speaks.
And remembering the birdsongs
Lightened many dreary hours,
As I plodded through the snowdrifts
Still recalling fields of flowers.

Moments spent in meditation
By a frosty windowpane,
And my eager heart grew restless
For the lilting song of rain.
How I languished for the sunlight
'Neath a brooding sky of grey,
For I held the springtime dearer,
Having been so long away.

Almost overnight it happened
As I knew that it would do,
As the dogwood blossoms opened
'Neath a cloudless sky of blue.
Heaven's feathered little singers
Filled the world with melody,
And I caught my breath in wonder,
. . . As April smiled at me!

Grace E. Easley

Spring Dreams

My dreams are not hindered
    by leaves;
they drift upward unhampered
    through budding
embroidery . . . O Fantasy,
    O Spring!

Eleanor Di Giulio

Thanks To Thee, O Lord Of Life

Thanks to Thee, O Christ victorious!
  Thanks to Thee, O Lord of Life!
Death hath now no power o'er us,
  Thou hast conquered in the strife.
Thanks because Thou didst arise
And hast opened Paradise!
None can fully sing the glory
Of the resurrection story.

Though I be by sin o'ertaken,
  Though I lie in helplessness,
Though I be by friends forsaken
  And must suffer sore distress,
Though I be despised, contemned,
And by all the world condemned,
Though the dark grave yawns before me,
Yet the light of hope shines o'er me.

Thou hast died for my transgression,
  All my sins on Thee were laid;
Thou hast won for me salvation,
  On the cross my debt was paid.
From the grave I shall arise
And shall meet Thee in the skies.
Death itself is transitory;
I shall lift my head in glory.

  Grant me grace, O blessed Savior,
  And Thy Holy Spirit send
That my walk and my behavior
  May be pleasing to the end;
That I may not fall again
Into Death's grim pit and pain,
Whence by grace Thou hast retrieved me
And from which Thou hast relieved me.

For the joy Thine advent gave me,
  For Thy holy, precious Word;
For Thy Baptism, which doth save me,
  For Thy blest Communion board;
For Thy death, the bitter scorn,
For Thy resurrection morn,
Lord, I thank Thee and extol Thee,
And in heaven I shall behold Thee.

Thomas Hansen Kingo, 1689

Rejoice

Rejoice for the risen Savior
Rejoice for the winter's end
Rejoice for the warmth of sunshine
Toward which all blossoms bend.

Rejoice with the brooks of springtime
Rejoice with flowers fair
Rejoice with a bird's loud caroling
Their glad tidings fill the air.

Rejoice with the holy women
Rejoice in their delight
Rejoice as they learn He has risen
In beauty, grace and might.

Helen Heberer

God's Bouquet

The world's a bouquet, a beauteous sight,
For flowers and trees in sunshine so bright
    Have grown, budded, bloomed,
    And in loveliness show
    God's hand in the earth
    And His glory below.
Knowing nothing but goodness, they answer
    God's call
Thus fulfilling their purpose, they live blessing all.

Edith Shubert

The forces of evil have always tried to bury goodness and truth and seal the grave with stones. We ask the same question as the women who went to the tomb of Jesus. Who will roll away the stones for us, of war, of hatred, of selfishness? Who will roll away the stones of despair, of doubt and fear, and finally, of death?

The women went to the tomb uncertain about how the stone might be removed, but they went in faith that it would be done. Their faith was rewarded, for when they looked up, they saw that the stone had been rolled back. When we are willing to approach the stones of life with faith, we, too, will discover that God does indeed roll them away. There is no burden or problem too heavy or too impossible to remove.

Donald B. Taylor

Spring

Spring blew an eddy
of spirea blossoms like
softly scented snow.

Miriam Woolfolk

The Burgeoning

It is blossomtime
But the fragrance,
The beauty, escape,
The promise unperceived
Except by those who seek,
And find.

It is blossomtime
Always, in the heart;
Buds of human kindness
Burgeon in many places . . .

Have you looked lately?

Mildred N. Hoyer

Mayflowers

Clusters of star petals
Dropped from on high,
Pink and white loveliness
Drawn from the sky;

Buried within their hearts
Phials of rare
Perfume distilled by God's
Angels in prayer;

Blossoms from heaven sent
Down to earth's sod,
To keep before mortals
The presence of God!

Dorothy M. Cahoon

God Is Near

Dogwood, redbud, new April green
Washed by spring's fresh showers clean,
Blossom-perfumed breezes rare
Whisper gently of God's care.
Clump of Sweet Williams, violets wild,
Singing birds, laughter of a child;
These combine in a message clear:
"God is near! God is near!"

Color-rimmed clouds near close of day,
Voices of children hard at play,
Evening star, night sounds in air—
All to remind us of God's care.
Our Father sees each bird in air,
He planned their notes so sweet and clear.
White lilies grow in beauty rare
Because God's love is everywhere.

Leota Campbell

LET'S READ IT TOGETHER
the children's corner

Bartholomew's Spring Surprise

Bartholomew Bunny
Playing out in the snow,
Wore earmuffs and scarf,
His pink nose all aglow,
Was romping and tossing snow
High in the air,
When he stooped to the ground
Very quickly, to stare.

He couldn't believe
What his twinkling eyes saw
Shining bright in the early day sun . . .
A tiny white blossom
With little leaves curled,
Indeed, spring's very first one.

Bartholomew shouted,
"Come look, come and see,
Spring has come
With her days warm and bright."
Mrs. Field Mouse,
In a kerchief and polka dot scarf,
Scampered close with a squeak of delight.

Mr. Crow cawed about
With much flapping of wings,
His top hat a little askew.
Sneezy Chipmunk who suffered
From bad winter colds,
Snuffled, "Springtime I welcome . . . kerchoo."

Otto Otter came sliding
Right over the bank
Of the half-frozen murmuring brook.
Mrs. Porcupine, wearing
Her best frilly cap,
Joined the group with her calendar book.

High in an oak tree
From his warm furry bed,
Flicker Squirrel
Poked his head out to see.
Chattered shrill with delight,
Said, "The time's about right!"
And flicked his tail vigorously.

Amid happy laughter
They all formed a ring
And sang a melodious air,
To welcome quite warmly
Spring's brave messenger . . .
A pretty white crocus, so fair.

Mildred L. Jarrell

34

Home and Family

The Attic

Don't you love an attic
On a windy, rainy day
Looking through the many things
You ought to throw away?

Here's a box of pictures,
Oh my word, just look at that!
Don't you *dare* remind me
I ever wore that hat!

Here's a dolly's cradle,
I can see her still
Rocking "baby" gently
"Sleep now, do be still."

Boxes, boxes everywhere
Wrapped in paper, tied with bows,
Some no longer labeled
Now what can be in those?

Memory sure is fleeting,
I can't remember when or where
I last saw these "treasures"
I wonder: Would I dare

Just close my eyes and toss things
Every spring and fall?
But then, my nice, neat attic
Wouldn't be fun at all!

Rhena S. LaFever

Well House, Sussex, England

I'm Burdened Down, Lord

Housewifing is a long and lonely task.
When I think about all the dishes I have yet to wash,
and the meals I have yet to cook,
and the beds to make, and the floors to mop,
the day-after-day, year-after-year jobs—
it's enough to make a body weep!
It is not just "oppressed by things undone,"
but oppressed by things yet to do!

Silly, isn't it! As though I really *had* to wash all the
future's dishes today.
You send us our days one at a time, Lord.
That is all we have to cope with.
Just *this* day. And really, it isn't half bad.
A normal number of normal chores—
and in between the chores, surprises!
Some I sandwich in myself, like a minute at the piano,
or a story with the kids.
Others just happen, but they brighten the day.

Housewifing is a challenge, Lord,
    and it *can* be a pursuit.

Forgive me my tedium.
Help me take charge of my days—
    and give them all I've got.
I shall make the tools of my trade implements of
    worship, and even as I stand at the stove,
        praise thee.

Amen

Jo Carr and Imogene Sorley

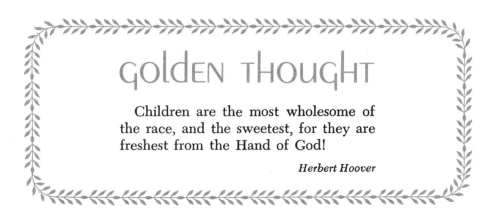

GOLDEN THOUGHT

Children are the most wholesome of
the race, and the sweetest, for they are
freshest from the Hand of God!

Herbert Hoover

In God's Pocket

The children used to play a game
On a gloomy, rainy day,
Of wishing they were someone else
Just to pass the time away.

Kay said a fairy she would be,
Asleep inside her locket!
"Not I," my Tim cried with disdain,
"I'll live inside God's pocket,

"And help Him when he sweeps the sky,
Turn the stars on every night,
And hang the clouds all out to dry,
Make the world below all bright!"

Lost little ones are surely there,
Helping God light up the sky,
And anyone who's lost a child
May look up and watch, as I.

Louise Justice

Secret World

Do children really live in a secret world of their own, a world that grown-ups once knew but can never quite find again? Sure they do! Every parent knows this, every teacher, every grown-up who has anything to do with kids.

It's a strange and wonderful world—half fantasy, half reality. The weather there is sunny mostly, but now and then there are storms. There's love in that world, and selfishness, and a surprising amount of violence, and sometimes fear. There's logic, too, although it gets oddly twisted at times. And magic. And more imagination than Jules Verne or Walt Disney ever dreamed of. And humor that any professional comedian would give his whole stable of gag writers for.

It's a world where nothing is predictable and nothing is commonplace because everything is fresh and unexpected and new. You can't describe it in so many words. You have to listen for it and watch for it....

Can grown-ups visit this secret world? I think they can. You don't need a passport or a visa or a formal invitation. All you need is a genuine love of kids and a little patience and understanding.

Art Linkletter

Going On Fifteen

We have a stranger in the house these days,
   A stranger with the most amazing ways!

He came one day, to both my grief and joy,
   The day I lost, somewhere, my *little* boy.

I never cease to marvel at him there—
   The length of him upon my small son's chair!

The overwhelming bigness of his feet,
   His clumsy, tender ways, so new, so sweet.

The way his hair stays combed! This much I know,
   My *little* son's wild mop was never so!

And when he speaks—stark wonder strikes my face.
   Wherever did he get that booming bass!

In all his dignity of fourteen years,
   I dare not ask him if he's washed his ears.

And so I take a furtive look, unseen,
   And find them both amazing pink and clean!

And, deep inside, it hurts a little so—
   The kind of hurt that only mothers know.

That dear, but dirty, little boy I had—
   He surely cannot be this spotless lad.

To watch his newfound charm beguile the girls,
   Remembering how he used to pull their curls;

I see him trying men's clothes on for size,
   And, somehow, there's a mist before my eyes.

But then I find my rifled cookie jar
   And know my *little* boy is not gone far.

Helen Lowrie Marshall

GOldEN NUGGET

You can't change the color of your child's eyes, but you can make them glow with the light of true love. Nothing gives the child greater security, and creates in him a greater reverence for others, than for him to receive and give love.

Billy Graham

My Two Daughters

Two lovely daughters the Lord blessed me with,
To love them with all of my might,
Oh, what an honor entrusted to me.
Dear Lord, let me bring them up right.

One angel arrived in the fall of the year
Then thirteen months later the other.
One girl has dark hair and looks like her dad,
The other is fair like her mother.

Now what shall I do in the job that is mine?
I'll teach them how chores can go faster,
But what shall I do about spiritual needs?
I'll enlist the help of the Master.

So I taught them of Jesus the best that I could
And I said, He's my friend till the end.
Soon they loved Him as I did, and it thrilled my heart
When they chose Him as their special Friend.

Then I taught them to bake and I taught them to sew,
And I taught them to honor God's Word.
Now they're just about grown, my work's almost done,
The rest of it's up to the Lord.

But I won't be worried when they're not with me.
For somehow I know they'll go right,
For I've taught them the good things the best that I could,
And loved them with all of my might.

Dee Gaskin

Mother

Have you ever stopped to wonder,
    What a queer old world 'twould be,
If there'd been no mother's kisses,
    If there'd been no mother's knee?

Have you ever stopped to ponder,
    As you pass down life's broad road,
Who'd have shouldered all the burdens,
    And your heavy, weighty load?

Take a moment just to ponder,
    Think how much she means to you,
Figure up on mother's ledger,
    Just how much you're over due.

Take a minute and just wonder,
    If life's road would be as smooth,
If there'd been no mother near you,
    None to love, caress and soothe.

Find the time sometime to write her,
    Tell her just how much you care,
Tell her that she's not forgotten,
    Tell her that your life is square.

For of all the things a mother
    Likes to think about her son,
It's to know he's straight and clean
    And manly — all rolled into one.

Have you ever stopped to wonder,
    What a hard life it might be,
If you'd never known a mother,
    Nor kneeled beside her knee?

Walter Scott Bewley

GOLdEN VERSE

Only One Mother

Hundreds of stars in the pretty sky,
Hundreds of shells on the seashore
* together,*
Hundreds of birds that go singing by,
Hundreds of lambs in the sunny weather.

Hundreds of dewdrops to greet the dawn,
Hundreds of bees in the purple clover,
Hundreds of butterflies on the lawn,
But only one mother the wide world over.

George Cooper

We Honor Mother

Time has scattered the snowy flakes on her brow, plowed deep furrows on her cheek, but is she not beautiful now? The lips are thin and shrunken, but these are the lips that have kissed many a hot tear from the childish cheeks.

The eye is dimmed, yet it glows with soft radiance of holy love, which can never fade. Ah, yes, she is a dear old mother.

The sands of time are nearly run out, but she will go farther, and reach down lower for you than anyone else on earth. You cannot walk in a midnight haunt where she cannot see you. You cannot enter a prison whose bars will keep her out. You cannot mount a scaffold too high for her to reach, that she may bless you in evidence of her deathless love.

When the world shall despise and forsake you, when it leaves you by the wayside to die unnoticed, the dear old mother will gather you up in her feeble arms and carry you home, and tell you of your virtues, until you almost forget that your soul is disfigured by vice.

Love your mother tenderly. Cheer her declining years with tender devotion. She is your total refuge.

Author Unknown

Flickering Flames Of Memory

Much has been written about sacred spots around the home place—the old oaken bucket, the old swimmin' hole, the old apple tree, and others. We had all these interesting and vital spots at our country home when I was a boy, but none equaled in influence and in precious memories the big fireplace that furnished the sole heat for the living room all through the cold Illinois winters.

Into this fireplace went our energies and our dreams, and out of it came wonderful stories of adventure and sacrifice. Each of us contributed to the life of the fireplace, but it contributed far more to our lives.

It required many swings of the axe and many drags of the crosscut saw to shape those mammoth backlogs and the smaller pieces of wood for the fireplace. Fingers often tingled from cold as they dug wood out of the snow, and chilly sensations ran up and down backbones as bits of snow rolled from the wood piled in our arms, onto upturned coat collars and slid down our backs. It took work to keep the big flames crackling and burning in the fireplace—but it was worth it!

Why do we so greatly enjoy the painting of a scene before a fireplace? It is always enticing. Is it because of the color and contrasts provided by the flickering fire and the shadows? Perhaps there is an appeal to our artistic senses, but I am inclined to believe it is because of the long thoughts which fire inspires and the associations that surround it.

There was a grandmother in our home. On long winter evenings Grandmother sat in her wicker rocker before the fire. Usually one of us was in her lap and two or three of us on the floor with our heads resting on her knees and our eyes toward the fire. Her black shawl with long fringe covered her shoulders, which had no heat to warm them. Ten feet from the fireplace was uncomfortable. Sometimes hours passed without anyone saying a thing. Grandmother's fingers went slowly through our hair or patted our cheeks in thoughtful rhythm. It was so comfortable. Grandmother liked it, and so did we.

Some evenings, however, we were not so peaceful. Happenings of the day or weather conditions provoked a restlessness that had to be met in a different way than with silences before the fireplace. Grandmother must tell a story—a story of real life as she knew it in England, as she knew it on the way across the great ocean, and as she found it when she reached the wonderful America. She told it in her simple way. There was nothing dramatic about Grandmother's delivery, but there was excitement in her story. She described the reaction when her father announced they were to sail for America. She told how they were received kindly in the United States, and how she grew to womanhood, met a young farmer from Kentucky, started their wedded life in Illinois; how they built the home in which Grandmother and we then lived, and how their children—Dad, Aunt Kate, Uncle John and Uncle Presley—came to make them happy. It was a long story and not always was it told in full in one evening, but it was told to us many times. Each time it grew in interest and Grandmother became more wonderful.

Sunday evenings before the fireplace were great occasions for the family. Then Dad was the storyteller, and none was better. The ordinary had to be converted into the extraordinary for Dad—a dog was always a lion, a wind was always a cyclone, something good was superb, and something bad was terrible. Mother was always shocked at the way he told us Bible stories.

"Why do you put all those flourishes on?" she would say. "The story is wonderful enough without you adding to it."

But, nevertheless, Dad's Moses and Dad's bullrushes were always better than anybody else's, and the Bible was made an interesting book. The morals he taught us from the stories were cleancut, and we couldn't forget them.

Fat Irish potatoes were buried in the hot ashes for a thorough roasting. Bread was toasted before the hot coals, and coffee simmered in a pot set between two chunks to keep it from tilting. The Sunday evening meal was prepared in the fireplace, and we partook of it on the hearth as the flickering flames cast shadows on the walls of the otherwise unlighted room

Old fireplace—teacher in contentment, in human love and sympathy, in concentration, in storytelling and in logical thinking—your memory will ever be cherished. I know that your influence was more than I am able to make evident. I will always be grateful for the joys you contributed and the ambitions you aroused. How can a man be anything worthwhile without the home ties that center so naturally and so effectively around the fireside?

Frank Warren Rucker

GOLDEN THOUGHT

I don't know who my grandfather was;
I am much more concerned to know
what his grandson will be.

Abraham Lincoln

Hands Of The Soil

Hands that are large and tough
   from years of rugged, outdoor work.
Hands with fingers sensitive to music,
   but too thick to strike just one key on the piano,
   or a single string on a violin.
Hands that are versatile,
   simultaneously wielding an ax
   and swiping a fistful of berries from a nearby bush.
Hands that clasp themselves habitually in prayer
   giving thanks for food, for rain, for sun,
   for late frosts, early springs, good yield,
   for soil, for health, for a newborn calf.
Hands that are strong,
   squeezing out a pailful of milk in just no time,
   pulling strands of barbed wire taut,
   carrying mountains of hay and oceans of water
   to hungry, thirsty farm creatures.
Hands that are gentle,
   marvelling at the softness of a furry kitten,
   rescuing a killdeer's nest from the path of the plow,
   patting the shoulder of a disappointed child.
Hands that are inventive,
   twisting, pounding, pinching until a machine is fixed,
   shaping an idea into something useful.
Hands that are wrinkled and tired
   from over a half century of tilling,
   planting, weeding, harvesting.
Hands that I love—
   a farmer's hands,
   my grandpa's.

Lois Mae Cuhel

She Didn't Do Much

I didn't do much, today, she said.
I just got breakfast and made the beds.
And washed the dishes an' swept the floors,
An' helped outside with a few little chores
Like feeding the chickens and milking the cow—
It didn't take very long anyhow.
Then I churned some butter an' set it to cool,
An' got the children off to school,
Except the baby and little Tom;
An' then I put the boiler on
An' heated some water an' washed a few
Of the baby's clothes, an' a dress or two
For the girls and me, an' some shirts for the men.
An' then it was time to start cooking again.
Of course the baby was bathed and fed
An' tucked away for a nap in bed.
Then little Tom fell and hurt his knee
An' there was no one to doctor it up but me;
Then I mended up his choo-choo train
An' got him started to playing again.
Then after dinner with dishes through
I worked in the garden an hour or two.
Then I ironed the clothes and hung them away
And painted a cupboard in blue and gray.
When the children came home from school at last
And had a wee lunch, it was four and past.
Then clothes must be changed and chores begun
An' a little errand to town be run.
When supper was over and dishes, too,
There was still a little mending to do.
Then I helped with lessons before 'twas late.
And got the children to bed at eight;
But somehow I'm tired anyway
Though I didn't do very much today.

M. L. Ford

Memory Making

Jake wondered if it really mattered. He waited while Billy scrambled out of the car, then picked up the bait bucket, basket, and stakes, and walked over the backwater where the weeds grew tall.

When you went out of your way to do something meaningful with a child, would he remember it at all? Last night they'd spent the evening out on the sand, the family all huddled in blankets, discussing the stars and the firmament. And what did Billy and his sister talk about at breakfast this morning? The shuttle train on the boardwalk, that's what.

"Are the crabs in there, Daddy?" Billy asked, pointing warily at the water in the inlet.

"Yep. Our supper's waiting, Billy. All we have to do is catch it."

The five-year-old settled himself on a rock, feet pulled up, and watched while Jake waded out ten yards and pushed the stakes down into the sandy earth.

"They're all in a row, Daddy! It looks like a fence!" Billy chortled happily, eager for a new experience.

Without answering, Jake took a ball of twine from his pocket and tied a long piece to each stake.

"Bring me the bait bucket, Billy," he called. "And the net."

Billy slid down off the rock, picked up the bucket of chicken wings and the long handled net, and walked to the water's edge, staring intently down into the water.

"Come on, before the crabs go somewhere else," Jake called jovially.

"I guess I don't want to," Billy replied.

Jake turned completely around. "Why? What's the matter?"

"I'm scared, Daddy."

"Of what?"

"A crab's gonna bite me."

"No, he's not, Billy. That's why you've got your sneakers on."

"He'll bite my sneakers."

"That won't hurt you. They're old shoes, anyway, Billy. Come on now, you came along to go crabbing."

In answer, Billy began to sob. "I'm afraid, Daddy! Come and get me."

Jake sloshed back to the bank, trying not to show his impatience.

"Carry me," Billy whimpered.

"No, Son, I'm not going to carry you. Once you get out there, you've got to stand in the water like real fishermen do." Jake picked up the bucket in one hand and the net in the other. "Look, I'll go first, and you step right where I do. Then if there's an old crab down there, I'll find him first and he'll bite me. Okay?"

"Okay, Daddy," Billy replied and clutched the belt on Jake's jeans.

Slowly they made their way awkwardly out to the stakes. Jake taking a step and lifting the other foot, Billy putting his own small foot in its place. Left . . . right . . . left . . . right . . . hold. . . .

The journey was over and Billy gave a deep sigh as he began to breathe more normally.

"Watch what I do now, Billy," Jake said. "Here. Hold the bucket." He tied a chicken wing to the loose end of each string and flung it as far out in the water as it would go.

"How come the crabs eat chicken?" Billy asked. "There aren't any chickens in the ocean."

That had never occurred to Jake. "Search me. Guess it's sort of like Sunday dinner to them. They don't get it often, so it's a special treat."

When the strings were baited, Jake took the bucket back to shore, then went out again to wait with Billy.

"How do we know when a crab starts eating it, Daddy?"

"Well, you have to keep checking, like this." Jake bent over and gave a gentle pull on one of the strings. It offered no resistance. "If a crab's on the other end, Billy, you can feel a little tug."

He tried another. Nothing. But the third line not only resisted but began moving sideways in the water.

"Hey! We've got a bite, Billy! The crab thinks it's a take-out restaurant and he's trying to carry the chicken home. Here." He handed the string to his son. "Now you pull it in slowly, like this. See? Not too fast . . . just . . . slowly . . . that's the way, sport, . . . keep pulling. . . ."

Jake took the net and inched out toward the bait. At that moment the chicken wing came into view, followed by a huge crab, and Billy gave an excited yell and jerked hard on the string. The crab dropped off before Jake could net it.

"Aw!" Billy said.

"That's okay, Son . . . that happens," Jake comforted. "A lot more get away than are caught. That's why we've got to work all afternoon to get enough for dinner. But you don't mind, do you?"

"Huh uh," Billy answered. "I don't care."

Thirty years ago, Jake and his father had crabbed in this very same inlet. "Used fish heads for bait then," Jake was thinking. "Yeah, and weights on the string. Should have a float too, though. Lets you know when a crab's got it. That's what I should have brought. A float."

Some of the crabs had got away then too, he mused, and his own father had reacted with patience and a sense of humor. Jake was glad he could pass that much on to his son. Maybe that's what Billy would remember about this day.

One of the lines pulled taut, and small bubbles rose to the surface.

"It's a bite!" Jake told his son again. "Pull it in, Billy. When you see the crab at the end, just keep pulling slow and steady. I'll do the rest."

Continued on page 50

Continued from page 49

With wide eyes and open mouth, the young boy began pulling the string. Now and then he would glance at his father for encouragement, and Jake would say, "You're doing fine, Billy. Easy, now."

It was an even bigger crab this time, and Billy closed his eyes so he wouldn't panic. With a sudden swoop, Jake thrust the net in the water, and the next moment the crab was hoisted into the air, its claws entwined in the net, the string, and the bait.

Jake whooped triumphantly and ran splashing back to the shore to dump their catch in the basket.

"We got one, Daddy! We got one!" Billy screeched, and the warmth of the afternoon sun settled down upon them as they took their places once again and waited.

The hours crept by. Like a heron in a marsh, Billy stood first on one leg, then the other, staring intently down in the water from time to time. Every so often the stillness was interrupted by another catch.

"Well, maybe we ought to quit after a while," Jake said finally, as he checked the basket. "How many crabs can you eat?"

Billy shook his head.

"Don't know?" Jake puzzled.

"I don't want any. I just like to help you catch 'em," Billy grinned.

Jake grinned back. "Never heard such a thing! Fisherman who doesn't like to eat! Well, there's plenty here. Let's go home, boy."

He waded back in to pull up the stakes. And then, with Billy following his footsteps behind, they took their gear to the car and slid gratefully onto the front seat, glad for a chance to sit down.

"What did you like best about this afternoon, Billy?" Jake asked.

"Guess," said Billy.

"When we got that first crab—that real big one?"

"Huh uh."

"No? When we threw out the lines again after we'd catch one?"

"No."

"When we quit and started home. I'll bet that's it."

"No, it's not."

"I give up. You tell me."

"When you went in first and let me walk where you stepped. That was the best part."

Jake stared out over the highway, over his two big hands resting on the wheel, so huge compared to Billy's. Whoever would have thought it had any meaning at all, and yet it did. Jake had shown the way, and Billy—trusting—had followed.

"May it always be so easy," Jake prayed, knowing it would not, and he could tell by the weight of Billy's head against his leg that his son was asleep.

Phyllis Reynolds Naylor

What Goes On Inside

It does not matter too much what the outside of a boy or girl looks like—any more than it matters what the outside of a house looks like. It is what goes on inside that counts. The grandest mansion in the country can be a very unhappy home, while the simplest cottage can be the happiest place in the world.

Author Unknown

Old Rockers

Old rockers tell a story
Of joy-rich days gone by
Of babies cuddled to a breast
To cease their hungry cry.
Of old, old couples on a porch
Rocking the long hours through
Deep in their thoughts of the yester-years
When their world was young and new.
The summer night is a drowsy time
And able to hypnotize
But the grandfather clock sounds a warning chime
And the rockers creak as they rise.
Then late in the deep of the winter's hush
The rockers, forsaken will sway,
As old eyes strain through the window pane
Ears tuned to the sound of a sleigh
That brings a bit of the snow-crisp night
Inside from the young out there . . .
And the old folks nod reminiscently
As laughter floats on the air.
Old rockers tell a story
Never die nor fade away
They stand as precious monuments
To a lovely yesterday.

Elizabeth M. Adams

Man To Man

Your mom is calling, little man,
So run right home, fast as you can!
She might not see 'neath all that grime
That you've had such a wondrous time,
Stalking pirates around the bend,
For treasure trove at river's end!

I'm almost sure she'll tan your hide
For using mud-banks as a slide,
Nor care one bit that Indians hid
And shot you full of holes, (they did?
And that's how pants and shirt were torn?
And how your foot picked up that thorn?)

Now scamper up the stairs, my lad,
No use to tell what fun you've had,
Just scrub real good and never mind,
Mom doesn't mean to be unkind!
She just don't know how good it feels
To be a mess from head to heels!

Nor how much fun it is to test
Your manly prowess at its best,
Hunting for bandits in the hills,
Ignoring scratches, bumps and spills—
The bravest lad in all the land—
But women just don't understand!

Louise Justice

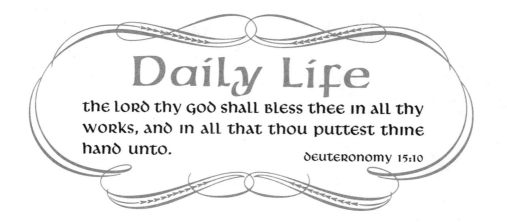

Daily Life

the lord thy god shall bless thee in all thy works, and in all that thou puttest thine hand unto.

deuteronomy 15:10

Reach To The Rose

Life has this dilemma
that hooks us on its horns:
Is the thornbush full of roses,
or the rosebush full of thorns?
Whatever is the answer
that living may disclose,
though fingers flinch at bleeding
I'll still reach to the rose.

Ralph W. Seager

My Symphony

To live content with small means;
To seek elegance rather than luxury,
   and refinement rather than fashion;
To be worthy, not respectable,
   and wealthy, not rich;
To study hard, think quietly, talk gently,
   act frankly;
To listen to stars and birds,
   to babes and sages, with open heart;
To bear all cheerfully, do all bravely,
   await occasion, hurry never;
In a word, to let the spiritual, unbidden and
   unconscious, grow up through the common
   —this is to be my symphony.

William Ellery Channing

What's A Table For?

It is 4:30 p.m. on a wilting August afternoon of tomato canning and pickle making. My closest neighbor and I suddenly meet face-to-face at the backyard swings where a shrieking battle between hers and mine has sounded the mother-alarm. The fight is put out shortly. But there we stand, half glad for the break.

"What are you having for supper?" she asks. Suppertime, more kitchen work, I think dismally. It's too hot today.

"Oh, some leftover casserole from last night's company—probably tomatoes again," is my answer. "What about you?"

"I have a pie and a few hot dogs. Let's put it together on the table!"

"About six o'clock, then. I'll put on the tablecloth."

The afternoon has a better feeling to it. The younger ones gather around now, at peace again, and the cry goes up, "We're eating together at the table tonight! Yippee!" In a second they climb the mimosa tree, swing wide from its branches, drop to the table and then to the lawn, and climb the tree again. It's a ritual of celebration.

Backyards in the old parts of eastern Pennsylvania towns are long and narrow. Two make a better yard than one. We completed the sharing of space by placing one good-sized picnic table in the middle under the shady mimosa tree. We set up a swing set on our side and a sandbox on theirs. A little garden straddles the line at the back edge of the yard. We both needed a lawn mower and it was a joint purchase.

Sharing the table has worked well for us. In two summers, there have been only a few occasions when both they and we wanted to entertain our separate guests at the same time at that table. A little shifting of plans to a park, indoors, or to another time solves those problems. Far more significant to us are the times when we together entertained mutual friends.

There are many summer weekends when one family is away and the other can entertain with the benefit of the whole yard. That's pleasant, too. We also frequently use the table alone as separate families. Looking out of the window near mealtime to see if they have set it or not before we go out with our things is about as formal as our arrangement has been, and it seems workable.

The table represents only a small segment of our lives being shared. But the idea grows.

We have dropped plans to purchase some things because we know they have one and we can use it. Many are the appliances, Sunday papers, folding chairs, dress patterns, books, tools, and toys that have crossed that narrow yard. With the material objects have come caring and counsel, baby-sitting help, closeness when husbands are away. Great is our joy in having close neighbors with whom to share a table.

Doris Longacre

Recompense

I have not seen the sea gulls
    swoop and soar
Nor heard the waves crash on
    a rock-bound shore;
I've never watched a lordly eagle fly
    in lonely grandeur
Caught twixt mount and sky;
I've never seen a golden tropic moon
    nor watched day break
    above a lush lagoon;
I've never heard a jungle tiger roar
    nor walked upon the ocean's sandy floor;
I've climbed no lofty mountain's
    grassy side
Nor ridden high above the prairie wide;
No fleecy cloudbank have I gazed upon
In close proximity to coming dawn;
No graceful ship has borne me
    atop the wave;
I've ne'er explored a subterranean cave . . .
. . . But I have seen the woods
    in early fall,
Garbed like gay gypsies
    for a festive ball;
I've watched ripe cornfields sway at noon
And bask in sunlight bronze
    as harvest moon;
I've spied the feathery maples
    in the spring
Catch rays of yellow sunlight
    on the wing;
I've heard the call of whippoorwill
    in flight
Whistle salute to fast approaching night;
I've known the gallant ghosts of ancient trees
Cradle the nests of homing birds and bees,
And seen the scampering woods squirrels
    frisk and play
'Mongst sere brown leaves
    at breaking of the day.
I've witnessed only simple, homely things,
Yet learned the joy that rich contentment brings.

Ruby A. Jones

Kneeling

God meant that we should kneel to do
The things that make life good,
To bathe the baby in his tub,
To polish fragrant wood.
To light a fire on the hearth,
To tend a flower-bed,
God didn't make us reach for these . . .
He made us kneel instead.

Carolyn Jerauld

The continuity of life is never broken; the river flows onward and is lost to our sight; but under its new horizon it carries the same waters which it gathered under ours, and its unseen valleys are made glad by the offerings which are borne down to them from the past—flowers, perchance, the germs of which its own waves had planted on the banks of Time.

Whittier

This Morning

If morning came but once
And did not come again,
What prodigies of light
    Would stun
Awakened men.
Wherefore, my eyes, so blind
To this enkindling sun?
This morning will not come again
For anyone.

Georgie Starbuck Galbraith

It's God's World

As long as the mockingbird greets the day with a song as the sun
    comes over the hill
and the whippoorwill calls from the wild wood when the day is
    spent and still
as long as violets peep through the earth and the wild rose blooms in
    June
as long as the trees inherit the earth, and the soft breeze whispers
    a tune,
It's God's world.

As long as man can glean the fields and ships go out to sea
as long as the rainbow appears after rain, God's symbol for all to see
as long as winter gives way to spring with a fresh new dress of green
as long as the seasons follow the years and the touch of God's hand
    is seen
It's God's world.

As long as the earth with children is blest with their joys and con-
    fusion and dreams
as long as the moon and stars at night from Heaven brightly beams
as long as the light goes on in our heart each time a loved one comes
    home
as long as the swallows return to build a nest in the old church dome
It's God's world.

As long as the gently falling rain calls forth the prairie to bloom in
    spring
as long as the willow tree bends in the wind and the road grows
    wider round the bend
as long as the brook flows on its way and darkness falls at close of
    day
as long as you hear a baby cry and a mother's soothing lullaby
It's God's world.

As long as a song can make the heart glad, as long as the good goes
    with the bad
as long as there's friendship and joy and gladness, as long as peace
    comes after sadness
as long as we live and toil the sod, as long as our faith is anchored in
    God
as long as we know when the last sun sets, it will rise again on Eternal
    rest
It's Still God's world.

Sylvia Schooler Brandt

I Remember

I remember wind blowing across fields of grass and ripening grain. As wave after wave rippled in the breeze I pictured myself at sea. If imagination were keen enough, I could actually turn a sickly green!

Grazing lands were dotted here and there by huge shade trees and the fields' boundaries were clearly defined by either stone or zig-zag rail fences. Hedgerows of choke cherry, elderberry and alders provided a safe and snug habitat for small game and pheasants. All this formed a mosaic, beautiful and pleasing to the eye. The pastures were given exclamation points of color by black and white bovine dominoes and fawn-colored Jerseys.

I remember the large vegetable garden in which weeds grew faster than the vegetables. Thick, green fingers of asparagus and rosy stalks of rhubarb were as true harbingers of spring as were the robins.

Down in the furthermost corner of the garden a little stream, scarcely wider than a hand, provided a natural bird bath and also a foot tub for horseradish roots which apparently liked wet feet. How the tears flowed when I was grating it!

How about the first strawberry shortcake of the season? Juicy, red berries, sun and vine-ripened, picked at their prime, washed, crushed and sweetened, then layered between and on top of buttery rounds of flaky biscuits? All this was topped off by heavy Jersey cream.

There were long rows of red and black raspberries, tangy red currants strung like rubies on slender stems hiding among green leaves and along one fence a row of huge blackberries. Mm-mm. Every day we checked the early "Yellow Transparent" apple tree to make sure the apples were "just right" for applesauce. The mere aroma of the ripe apples made us want to speed them on their way to the kettle.

Across the road were two red sour cherry trees and it was always a race to see who got there first . . . the robins or us! Later in the season came the Green Gage and Lombard plums and how "yummy" from the tree! We must have kept the pear trees just for the blossoms for they certainly were not exerting themselves as far as fruit was concerned.

In due time there were green and yellow beans, tall pole limas, carrots with feathery crowns, blood-red beets, spinach and golden corn. Tomatoes of all sizes filled baskets to overflowing. Cabbage and cauliflower heads grew larger by the minute and some actually burst with pride! A season was lost if we didn't have peas and new potatoes by the 4th of July. Speaking of potatoes, remember the dainty little yellow and white blossoms and the very "un-dainty" little bugs that had to be paddled off into a can of kerosene?

Cucumbers of all sizes and shapes hid under rough, fuzzy leaves, seemingly to appear out of nowhere. The "babies" went into a creamy mustard pickle and the larger ones were shared with any and all who would take them after a large crock in the cellar had been filled. The cucumber's cousin, the squash, roamed wherever fancy dictated. Often it sought companionship among the little pumpkins which refused to stay "little" and like Topsy, "jes' growed."

The white frame house with red roof was bordered, front, back and sides, by a kaleidoscope of color from early spring to late fall. Snowdrops, crocuses, lily-of-the-valley, hyacinths, bleeding hearts, pansies, coral bells, lilacs, iris and peonies took the spotlight until roses, geraniums, zinnias, marigolds, asters and hydrangeas demanded their time to be admired. Long window boxes were filled with colorful petunias and trailing ivy. Sweet peas grew on a trellis by the woodshed door (and the woodshed was more than a place to store wood!)

Mock oranges and yellow roses mingled their fragrances for the occupants of the first floor bedroom to enjoy and a peach tree stood as sentinel nearby. A gnarled old apple tree was left, unsightly as it was, in the backyard. Where else could one climb, swing, or hide?

Colorful sugar maples graced the front yard in Autumn and stood as guardians over the only "home" they had ever known throughout other seasons of the year. A poplar stood tall and straight with silvery "coins" twinkling in the breeze.

Where does one stop when memory pushes yet another memory to the forefront of the mind? Playing "Hide-and-seek" as a child among the stacked bales of hay high in the loft . . . swinging from long ropes, then dropping into huge mounds of soft hay or straw only to pop up looking for all the world like the scarecrow in the "Wizard of Oz."

Do children still rattle the latch on the hen-house door (less the hens be frightened) and then gather the fresh and often still warm eggs?

Do they know how to fill a kerosene lamp, carefully trim its wick and even more carefully wash and polish the clear glass chimney? Or polish a kitchen range?

Do they know the fun of a box supper? Can a child today watch Jack Frost paint a beautiful picture on an upstairs window pane in mid-winter, or hurriedly gather up his clothes and race downstairs to dress where it is warm near the old coal-burning "parlor" stove? Can he have for his "very best" friends a long-legged colt, a fuzzy newborn calf or a woolly lamb? Some can, but too few. Can he enjoy the sight and smell of homemade bread, pies, cakes and cookies for every-day fare? Or watch "Mommie" quilt? Can he ever experience a "sugaring off" party where maple sap was magically turned into maple syrup or maple sugar? In the cold and snow of an early spring evening, sitting near the big bonfire and steaming vats of fragrant syrup one could scarcely wait for "samples" to be served with hot biscuits. All accompanied by much laughter and singing.

It is good to remember!

Rhena S. LaFever

I Thank Thee, God

I cannot thank Thee, God, enough
For this small plot of ground, this roof,
These lifted walls that close me in
And hold me tenderly; this proof
Of Thy kind care for my great need
Of shelter and of daily bread;
But oh, there are no written words,
There are no words that have been said
That could express my gratitude
For the companionship of Love
That shares my simple fare—dear God,
A gift I would be worthy of!
And I would thank Thee for the tasks:
A fire to tend, a loaf to bake,
A floor to sweep, a seam to sew,
A clean, white-sheeted bed to make,
A lamp to light at evening time—
I thank Thee, God, for all of these;
For home, my home—for every home—
I thank Thee, God, upon my knees.

Author Unknown

GOLDEN NUGGET

Every man has a train of thought on which he rides when he is alone. The dignity and nobility of his life, as well as his happiness, depend upon the direction in which that train is going, the baggage it carries, and the scenery through which it travels.

Joseph Fort Newton

My Father's Church

Down a winding, dusty road, beside a gentle stream;
My father's church is nestled among my childhood scenes.
No stately cathedral is my father's church,
      not a modern building of glass—
Just a small white church, built with loving hands,
      on a field of soft green grass.

Most of the folks who worshiped there earned their living from
      the land;
Yet they were never too busy to lend a helping hand.
They served our Lord with gladness and practiced his Golden Rule;
Ofttimes they walked a mile or more to church and Sunday school.

I can still hear the church bell ringing and see the happy throng,
As the choir breaks forth in singing one of the glad old songs—
"Amazing Grace, How Sweet the Sound," "The Old Rugged Cross"
      on a hill.
If I close my eyes and listen, I can hear them singing still.

One day I returned to the small white church and viewed the
      peaceful scene;
Once more I walked down the winding road and stood by the
      gentle stream.
The bell was silent on my return, no sound of the choir's glad song;
yet in a corner of my heart they echo LOUD and STRONG.

Juanita C. Beard

The Last Haircut

With the retirement of a barber I had patronized for 12 years in Chicago, I faced the necessity of finding a new one among the three small shops in suburban Glen Ellyn, Ill., where I lived. I selected a shop next to the movie theater mainly because it happened to be a convenient place to park.

It was a fortunate choice. The shop was bright, clean, and well-equipped. Its two barbers not only were skillful tradesmen, they were friendly, personable, and interesting conversationalists.

The one who was destined to become "my barber" had wavy red hair, a clear complexion, and a kind expression, especially in his eyes. I guessed him to be in his early to mid-30s, but learned later he was somewhat older.

In our first confab, I discovered that barbering was only one of Red's several talents and interests. He also served from time to time as a substitute school-bus driver; he was known as "Mr. Fixit" by many of his neighbors; and he taught a Sunday-school class.

I learned about the latter when I slid 50¢—my usual tip—into Red's hand.

When he offered to return the two quarters to me, I told him I was accustomed to giving the tip in the city and was delighted to express my appreciation for his excellent work.

"Well, if you insist, I'll accept it and put it in the poor fund," Red said. He must have realized I thought he was joking, because he quickly added: "I really will put it to good use. The Sunday-school class I teach contributes all year to a special fund, and then at Christmastime we buy food and distribute baskets to as many needy families as we can."

Red remembered me when I returned four weeks later. It happened to be my birthday, and this led to a chat about our families. He told me he had a 21-year-old stepson, legally adopted, plus three children of his own, and he spoke lovingly of all four.

Red also told me he and his family lived quite a distance from Glen Ellyn, and he drove nearly 80 miles a day to and from work. I didn't learn the reason for this until a month later.

As he was finishing my haircut, Red used his comb to lightly tap a mole-like growth in front of my right ear.

"How long have you had this?" he asked casually. I said I had first noticed it several months earlier and assured him that it didn't hurt, never bled, and wasn't growing.

"Why don't you have it checked out anyway, just to be on the safe side?" were Red's parting words that day.

During my next visit with Red, the day before Father's Day, we discovered that both of us had lost our fathers at an early age. Red's mother also had died when he was quite young. He said he felt he had been fortunate in compensating for his lack of parents by helping care for his wife's mother and father in their declining years. After they died, Red and his wife had "adopted" two elderly couples and had helped care for them ever since. He said this was why he had not been able to move his family to a new location, even though his work sometimes took him far afield.

As he finished cutting my hair, he moved to the front of the chair, bent down to view the "mole" on my cheek at close range, then looked me squarely in the eye.

"I'm going to talk to you like a father," he said rather somberly. "I want you to have a doctor look at this thing without any more delays."

Another month passed. This time, as I was leaving the shop, Red followed me to the front door. "My friend, I've just given you the last haircut I'm going to give you," he said quietly. "Unless you have a doctor examine that growth, I don't want you to come back."

I looked at him, and there wasn't a trace of a smile on his face, only a look of concern and compassion.

Although I felt a little angry at what I considered Red's high-handed airs, I decided I'd have a doctor look at the mole "one of these days." I told my wife about the encounter I'd had with "that loquacious barber," and on the following Monday she calmly announced she had made an appointment for me to see our doctor on Thursday evening.

The doctor examined the lump and made arrangements immediately for me to enter the hospital "for either a biopsy or an excision." A sizable tumor was removed on August 15 and the laboratory tests revealed malignancy. The surgeon said it was fortunate that I had come for help when I did.

And so in early September I went back to the barber shop, not only because I needed a haircut but also because I wanted to thank Red. Upon entering the shop, I was amazed to find the two barber chairs and all the equipment were gone. Workmen were installing new carpeting, shelves, and other store fixtures. The workmen told me the barber shop had quietly ceased operation on August 15, to be replaced by a gift shop. They had no idea where Red and his partner had gone.

I made inquiries at nearby business firms, at the two other barber shops in the village, and among friends. I even called the local newspaper office and the telephone company for information. No one could tell me what had become of Red. He had simply disappeared from the local scene.

Wherever he is today, I hope Red is continuing to carry on his good work. I shall always feel certain that he had at least one important mission to fulfill in Glen Ellyn. He filled it well.

Cholm G. Houghton

golden thoughts

We find in life exactly what we put into it.

Emerson

I don't think much of a man who is not wiser today than he was yesterday.

Abraham Lincoln

Two friends walked home from work together. Each evening one bought his paper from a particular newsboy. He consistently greeted the boy with a kind word and a gracious thank you. The newsboy was as consistent in his grunting and growling in reply.

"How is it," his friend asked, "that you continue to speak so kindly to such a ruffian? He treats you like dirt. Yet, you purchase your paper from him and always express your thanks."

"It would be foolish to let a newsboy determine for me how I should act," replied the other. "I know how I ought to act. To do differently is reaction."

John M. Drescher

The Business

I missed You
this morning
Lord.
You were there.
 I wasn't.
I was too busy
 too soon.

Ida Barton

66

Time

Time.

It hangs heavy for the bored, eludes the busy, flies by for the young, and runs out for the aged.

Time.

We talk about it as though it's a manufactured commodity that some can afford, others can't; some can reproduce, others waste.

We crave it. We curse it. We kill it. We abuse it. Is it a friend? Or an enemy? I suspect we know very little about it. To know it at all and its potential, perhaps we should view it through a child's eyes.

"When I was young, Daddy was going to throw me up in the air and catch me and I would giggle until I couldn't giggle any more, but he had to change the furnace filter and there wasn't time."

"When I was young, Mama was going to read me a story and I was going to turn the pages and pretend I could read, but she had to wax the bathroom and there wasn't time."

"When I was young, Daddy was going to come to school and watch me in a play. I was the fourth Wise Man (in case one of the three got sick), but he had an appointment to have his car tuned up and it took longer than he thought and there was no time."

"When I was young, Grandma and Granddad were going to come for Christmas to see the expression on my face when I got my first bike, but Grandma didn't know who she could get to feed the dogs and Granddad didn't like the cold weather, and besides, they didn't have the time."

"When I was young, Mama was going to listen to me read my essay on 'What I Want to Be When I Grow Up,' but she was in the middle of the 'Monday Night Movie' and Gregory Peck was always one of her favorites and there wasn't time."

"When I was older, Dad and I were going fishing one weekend, just the two of us, and we were going to pitch a tent and fry fish with the heads on them like they do in the flashlight ads, but at the last minute he had to fertilize the grass and there wasn't time."

"When I was older, the whole family was always going to pose together for our Christmas card, but my brother had ball practice, my sister had her hair up, Dad was watching the Colts, and Mom had to wax the bathroom. There wasn't time."

"When I grew up and left home to be married, I was going to sit down with Mom and Dad and tell them I loved them and I would miss them. But Hank (he's my best man and a real clown) was honking the horn in front of the house, so there wasn't time."

Erma Bombeck

Left Behind

Lindy opened one eye slowly. She felt stiff and sore from sleeping on the hard seat. She looked around. Why was it so dark and quiet? As her eyes began to see better in the dark she could make out the big white screen on the wall. Why she was still at the City Museum! Her school class had spent the afternoon there. The last thing Lindy could remember was watching a film about the stars. She had fallen asleep and the rest of the class had gone and left her behind.

Lindy sighed. Why hadn't they awakened her? If her best friend, Tammy, had been in school today, this wouldn't have happened. But Tammy was home in bed with the mumps.

Well, the first thing she'd better do was find the others, Lindy decided. She walked carefully through the long rows of seats to the other side of the room. The big steel doors were closed. "That's why it seems so quiet," Lindy thought. She turned the knob and pushed the heavy door open.

She stood a moment in the doorway thinking. Where had Miss Ransom said the class would go after the film? The museum was so large it might take a while to find the rest of the class. Why had they turned the lights off? Lindy wondered. She felt scared. Maybe the class was already at the door, waiting for her. She didn't know how long she had been asleep. If she was late and holding the others up, her teacher would be upset with her. She turned and began running toward the main doors with the red EXIT signs over them.

"Miss Ransom!" She shouted into the silence. Where were all the people that always filled the museum? "Where is everybody?"

Lindy ran faster. The shadows around her seemed to be closing in, reaching out to touch her. Her heart pounded so hard she could feel its throb in her throat. Why didn't anyone answer her?

There was no one in sight when Lindy reached the big glass doors at the entrance. No cars were parked along the sidewalk, and the big yellow school bus which had brought the class was no longer waiting. All she could see through the glass was darkness. It was night!

Lindy sighed. Well, that was that. Miss Ransom and the class had gone back to the school and left her. The museum guides, the lady who sold the little sea horses and shells at the booth, the curator, and

68

even the janitor had gone home for the night. The museum was locked up tight.

What could she do? Lindy wondered. Would she just have to wait until the curator came to open the museum in the morning? Lindy looked up at the clock on the wall. It was too dark to see the hands, but her stomach told her that it was way past dinner time.

Why hadn't her mother and father come looking for her? They would miss her as soon as she didn't come home. By now they should have called the school to find out where she was. Miss Ransom would know that she hadn't ridden the bus back to the school. Her teacher always counted noses when they went on a class trip.

Lindy sat huddled on a stone bench. She was hungry, and her stomach just wouldn't be quiet. She wasn't really frightened, just sort of cold. If it was light, it would be fun to explore the museum.

She *would* go exploring! There was enough light from the moon coming in the high windows so she could see pretty well. First she would look at the rock display. It was her favorite. She loved the shiny black and smaller topaz and aqua-colored stones. She had even started a rock collection of her own at home.

Next, she would go to the exhibit where the "Clothes of Yesteryear" were worn by the wax family. It would be fun to cross under the chain and stand on the platform with the figures in their dresses of long ago. She would be very careful, but she wanted to feel the mother's and daughter's dresses of fine silk and velvet, and touch the soft looking white fur muff the little girl carried.

Saving the best for last, she would go to the park square up on the third floor. There in the midst of the velvet green lawn was a beautiful carriage drawn by four prancing black horses. What fun it would be to sit in the coach with the two footmen standing on the back and the driver up on the box, pretending that she was a grand lady.

Well, why not? Lindy smiled. She wasn't really afraid. As long as she had to stay in the museum, she might as well have fun.

Lindy stood up and started toward the rock cases. She knew her way around, even in the dark. She and her parents had visited the museum many times.

The rocks looked different without the showcase lights on them. The moonlight shining in the windows cast a magical glow on the colored stones. Lindy wished she could touch the lovely rocks, but she knew she wouldn't if she could. Some things were just for looking at. She smiled again. The best part about being all alone in the museum was that there was no one to say "hurry up," or "come along, now." She could look as long as she liked.

Lindy had a lot of fun pretending to be a member of the wax family. She was just heading upstairs for the Park Square when a jangling noise pierced the silence. It was a telephone! As the phone kept ring-

Continued on page 70

Continued from page 69

ing, Lindy ran toward the noise coming from near the souvenir booth.

The phone was high on the wall over a glass case. Lindy hurried behind the case and reached to answer it, but she couldn't reach the receiver. She looked around for something to stand on. The phone rang again and again. If she stood on her tiptoes she could just barely touch the mouthpiece. She took a deep breath and jumped, at the same time tugging on the cord. The receiver fell off and landed on the case top with a thud. Lindy grasped the phone to her ear.

"Hello! Hello!" she shouted into the mouthpiece, but there was no answering voice. The phone line was dead.

Lindy slowly laid the receiver on the case top. She hadn't gotten it down in time. Now the phone was off the hook and no one could call again unless she could find a way to hang the receiver back up. She looked up and down the aisles, but she couldn't find even a small box or stool that she could stand on.

Sadly Lindy walked back to the stone bench and sat down. She was getting cold again, and she wished she hadn't left her sweater in the school bus. What difference did it make if no one could call her? Maybe if they tried and the phone gave a busy signal, they would know someone was in the museum and come to see who it was.

The moon shone brightly through the glass doors now, but for Lindy the magic of the museum was gone. She lay down on the cold stone bench and slowly the tears began to run silently down her cheeks.

She was so unhappy. Then she remembered! God knew where she was. He had known all the time. He could help her mother and father to find her. She closed her eyes and prayed.

"Please, God, help Mother and Dad to come after me. Please?"

Suddenly bright lights were shining in her face. Two policemen and people from the museum were asking all sorts of questions. Her mother and father and Miss Ransom were all trying to hug her at once.

"Lindy, we've been looking all over for you! We've been so worried!" her mother exclaimed.

"I wasn't lost, I just fell asleep during the film and everyone left me," Lindy explained sleepily. "I was here all the time, just waiting."

"It was all my fault, Lindy," Miss Ransom said. "I made a horrible mistake when I counted the children on the bus. We had a visitor today, and I forgot to add one more to the number of pupils even with Tammy home ill with the mumps. I don't know how I could have made such a dreadful mistake."

"That's okay." Lindy smiled. "I asked God to help you find me."

Her father smiled, "Ready to go home?"

Lindy nodded. She had almost forgotten about being cold and frightened. She just wanted to go home, eat her dinner and be tucked into her own bed.

Sharon B. Miller

American Heritage

WHERE THE SPIRIT OF THE LORD IS,
THERE IS LIBERTY.

II CORINTHIANS 3:17

First Prayer In Congress

O Lord, our Heavenly Father, High and mighty King of kings, our Lord of lords, who dost from Thy throne behold all the dwellers on earth and reignest with power supreme and uncontrolled over all the Kingdoms, look down in mercy, we beseech Thee, on these American States, who have fled to Thee from the rod of the oppressor, and thrown themselves on Thy gracious protection, desiring henceforth to be dependent only on Thee; to Thee, they have appealed for the righteousness of their cause; to Thee do they now look up for that countenance and support which Thou alone canst give; take them therefore, Heavenly Father, under Thy nurturing care; give them wisdom in Council and valor in the field; defeat the malicious designs of our cruel adversaries; convince them of the unrighteousness of their cause; and if they persist in their sanguinary purpose, O let the voice of Thine own unerring justice, sounding in their hearts, constrain them to drop the weapons of war from their unnerved hands in the day of battle!

Be thou present, O God of wisdom, and direct the councils of this honorable assembly; enable them to settle things on the best and surest foundation. That the scene of blood may be speedily closed; that order, harmony and peace may be effectually restored, and truth and justice, religion and piety prevail and flourish among Thy people. Preserve the health of their bodies and the vigor of their minds; shower down on them, and on the millions they here represent, such temporal blessings as Thou seest expedient for them in this world, and crown them with everlasting glory in the world to come. All this we ask in the name and through the merits of Jesus Christ, The Son, our Saviour.

AMEN

*Independence Hall,
Philadelphia, Pennsylvania*

73

Beauty Queen

A beauty contest for flags;
Old Glory wins first place!
No other banner matches
Its proud, symbolic grace.

Ethel P. Travis

Profile Of Lincoln

An editorial profile of Lincoln appeared in the Chicago Tribune five days before he was nominated in 1860:

"Mr. Lincoln stands 6 feet 4 inches. His frame is gaunt and wiry. In matters of dress he is by no means precise. Always clean, he is never fashionable. He is careless, but not slovenly.

"In manner he is remarkably cordial and, at the same time, simple. His politeness is always sincere but never elaborate and oppressive.

"His gains from his profession [as a lawyer] have been moderate, but sufficient for his purposes. While others have dreamed of gold, he has been in pursuit of knowledge.

"In all his dealings he has the reputation of being generous, but exact, and above all, he is religiously honest, and lives at peace with himself."

Martin Buxbaum

God Bless Our Land

God bless the flag that flies above,
And keep its colors glorious;
Lead on, lead on, in war or peace,
Let Freedom reign, victorious!

God bless the land the Pilgrims trod,
God bless each great endeavor,
And keep her, Lord, the land of hope,
Forever—and forever!

Louise Weibert Sutton

O God, Our Father, Ruler Of All Nations

O God, our Father, Ruler of the Nations,
The Leader of our country from its start:
How richly you have blessed us, beyond measure!
We come to you with full and grateful hearts:
O help us now to wisely use our plenty.
Forgive us for our greed and for our waste,
And teach us how to share what you have given,
Till poverty and hatred be erased.

Around us are the forces of corruption,
Our vision fails, direct us by your hand.
Inspire in us the faith that led our fathers,
And guided them to found this mighty land.
Our leaders need your courage and your wisdom,
O speak again through men whose lives are just,
Until your will is done across this nation,
And we can truly say, "In God we trust!"

We thank you that our land is blest with freedom,
This testing ground for true democracy.
And pray that in the course of human struggle,
We'll always stand for truth and liberty.
For here the cries of dissidence and protest
Can mingle with the rousing shouts of praise.
But in this very freedom, grant us wisdom
to keep your laws and serve you all our days.

America, the beautiful, the mighty,
America, the land of liberty!
O, Father, keep us mindful of our blessings,
And never let us turn away from Thee.
Surround us with your cleansing, healing Spirit.
Forgive our sin and purge our apathy.
Now use us as an instrument of blessing
To all the Earth—America, the Free!

Mrs. Moncrief Jordan

The Old Soldier

For a long time after the Revolution, the little settlement of Sunmore had made a great day out of the Fourth of July. People there had not forgotten what it meant. As the years went by, a set form grew up for the day's celebration. At dawn, the big boys fired the old cannon which stood on the village common. There was a meeting about eleven in the morning at the Town Hall, where people made speeches and sang patriotic songs. After that, a picnic lunch was eaten out on the green. Then the procession formed to escort the old soldiers out to the Burying Ground where they put flags and flowers on the graves of their comrades who had been soldiers in the Revolution.

Nearly everybody in town marched in this procession, carrying flags and flowers. The boys especially looked forward to this celebrating because it was like passing a milestone on the road to growing up when you were given a chance to join in the cannon-firing.

With the passing years, the Sunmore men who had been in the Revolutionary Army grew older and older, fewer and fewer. Dr. White carried the veterans in his own chaise behind his ancient roan horse. Besides being the local expert on medicine, which was to be expected, Dr. White was also the specialist on local history.

When May ended and June began in 1848, seventy-one years after the Battle of Bennington, people began to plan as usual for the Fourth of July celebration. But now there were no old soldiers to be found. For the past five years there had been only two, both of them very old. Now both were gone. Without even a solitary veteran how could people remember what the Fourth of July was really about?

Andrew Bostwick heard his family lamenting that the celebration wouldn't be much without the old soldiers in it to connect the town with the Revolution. He was a bright boy of ten and he had listened to plenty of stories about the Battle of Bennington. He was just beginning to be old enough to help fire off the cannon and to hand flowers to the old soldiers in the cemetery. And now there weren't any old soldiers!

One day in June he was sent out to look for a lost cow which hadn't come back to the barn from the mountain pasture. Up there he met a school mate, Will Hunter. The two boys sat down on a ledge to have a talk. Before long Andrew brought out what was weighing on his mind . . . the Fourth of July celebration without any old soldiers. Will told him, "There's an old fellow lives in Hawley Hollow. Maybe he fought in the Revolution. He's old enough anyhow."

"That's not in Sunmore," Andrew objected. "We have to have a sure-'nough Sunmore soldier for our Fourth."

"Is, too, in Sunmore." Will was positive. "His folks vote in our

Town Meeting, all right."

So there was to be a genuine Revolutionary soldier after all for the Fourth of July celebration. And who had found him? Why, Andrew Bostwick and William Hunter, two little boys. The Program Committee arranged that during the meeting they were to stand on the platform on each side of the old soldier, and to march in the procession just in front of Dr. White's chaise. They were to be called the "Young Guard of Honor." Those boys could hardly wait for the Fourth of July!

On the morning of the Fourth, Andrew's father drove his farm wagon up into the Hollow to fetch the old man. A crowd was waiting in front of the Town Hall when they got back. They began to clap and cheer when Mr. Bostwick helped lift the bent old man out of the wagon and led him into the Hall. Andrew and Will, the Young Guard of Honor, carried his ancient gun in and put it across his knees.

The crowd came into the Town Hall, took their seats and began fanning themselves. The chorus did not begin to sing, for at this point Dr. White, who always sat on the platform, called out to Andrew, "Here, let me look at that gun!" Andrew was surprised. He put his hand on the gun, and leaning down, to the old man's ear, said to him as loudly as he could, "Dr. White wants to see your gun."

The doctor took a sharp look at it, then put on his glasses and looked very carefully at a certain place near the trigger. Everybody wondered what was on his mind.

When he looked up, his face was all astonishment. "This is a German gun! The old man must have been one of those Hessians who fought against the Americans!" A Hessian! He had fought on the other side. People's mouths dropped open, they were so taken aback.

The old man hadn't heard any of this because he was so deaf. He sat quietly, his gentle old eyes looking around at the people in the hall. For a minute nobody could think what to say. Or what to do.

Then Andrew ran out to the front of the platform and began to talk very fast. "Listen," he said, "that was seventy years ago. No matter how mad you are at somebody, you don't keep it up forever. The Bible says not to. He's lived close to us all that time, and farmed like anybody, and paid his taxes. He's old. It would be *mean* of us to . . ."

Andrew had never even spoken a piece in school. When he realized what he was doing, he stopped talking and hung his head. He went back and put one hand on the old man's shoulder. The wrinkled face lifted to smile at him. Andrew smiled back. But his lips were trembling.

People began to rustle and move their feet. But when Dr. White stood up to say something, they were still again. "It comes back to me now," he said. "I remember reading in one of those old books in my collection that some of the Hessians, too badly wounded to be moved, were cared for in near-by farmhouses, and a few of these are supposed

Continued on page 78

Continued from page 77

to have stayed in Vermont. That's all the history book said. Jim Hale told me the rest. He couldn't say about more than one. But one, he was sure of. The day after the battle a young Hessian, pretty badly wounded, was found unconscious in the woods . . . carried into a farmhouse. By the time he was well enough to get around, there weren't any soldiers or armies left in those parts. So the family let him stay on with them. While Mr. Hale didn't know any more for sure, he thought the young Hessian moved away into the back country . . . he'd never heard just where." The doctor took a long breath before he went on. "I believe I know where he went . . . and where he is. He's right on this platform." The doctor still had the old rifle in his hands. He turned around now and laid it back on the old man's knees. Then he faced the audience. "I also believe young Andrew Bostwick had the right idea. Seventy years *is* too long to keep on bearing a grudge. I think we'd better go ahead with our celebration. Maybe the Reverend Hardwick might have something to say about this."

The old man from Hawley Hollow had evidently supposed that it was all part of the program . . . that the doctor had been making one of the planned speeches. Now, seeing the minister step forward in his black clergyman's clothes, he thought the prayer was to be said. He leaned forward in his chair and dropped his eyes to the ground.

As a matter of fact, Reverend Hardwick did pray. He was silent a long time. Then he said, "May war pass and peace be with us. Amen."

He sat down. The Moderator of the Town took his place. He said soberly, "I think this is something we ought to take a vote on." In his big official voice he announced, "The question before this house, as I see it, is: has the Revolutionary War ended? Or is it still going on?"

They all sat still. The deaf ears of the old soldier had, of course, not heard any of this. His hands lay thin and knotted on the arms of his chair. His clean old face was calm. He smiled a little.

A man stood up and said, "Mr. Moderator, I move you that the celebration proceed as planned."

Several voices said, "I second the motion."

Then the vote was taken. Everybody voted "Aye."

So, that afternoon, when the usual speaking and singing had been done, and the picnic lunch eaten out on the Common, the procession formed as usual, to march out to the cemetery.

The old soldier looked very tired by this time, but still cheerful. He came out of the Town Hall on Dr. White's arm, and was helped up into the chaise. The Young Guard of Honor held their flags high. The little girls in white dresses were pushed by their mothers into line, two by two. The men and women formed, four by four. The doctor slapped the reins over the old horse's back.

"Forward, *march!*" cried the bandmaster. And away they all went.

Dorothy Canfield

Two Hundred Years

'Cross trackless plains men laid new paths
   That led to peace and hope.
To uncleared forests settlers came
   With families, to grope
For freedom, and to flee from deep
   Oppression, want and woe.
They found our land—America,
   Two hundred years ago.

They fashioned well, those austere men.
   America became
A haven for those men who sought
   New vistas they could tame.
They did not seek security,
   Nor nooks devoid of fears.
The land they made now celebrates
   Its first two hundred years.

The future is a trackless plain,
   Where men have never trod.
It beckons to America
   To keep its trust in God
And, like our fathers, brave and tame
   Each challenge, as it nears.
That free men's feet may blaze new trails
   The next two hundred years!

Dwayne Laws

Independence Day

We, the people, speak —
We speak of *our land*,
This land we call
The United States of America,
Won by the blood of our forefathers
Because they loved freedom.
To our land came those of many nations
Who also loved freedom.
With energy and hope and faith
They worked and built,
With faith in themselves and faith
       in their God
Whom they worshipped as they pleased.

What few short years have passed,
Beginning from the wilderness
To the broad and prosperous land of today,
The great cities filled with people
Working and hoping to reach the same end —
       Happiness.

The tradition and beauty of New England,
The broad expanse of mid-country —
Prairies, wheat fields, industries,
       great rivers;
The lush beauty of the tropic South;
Mountains — wooded, green mountains,
Thick with towering trees;
Stark, barren mountains
Tipped with the eternal snows,
Core of the earth's heart
Tossed out by violent Nature.

Broad, dry deserts
Filled with death
But waiting for life,
Thirsty for the living water,
Brought by man's ingenuity
To blossom and fulfill.

The West, the Big West —
The highest mountains, the lowest deserts,
The largest trees;
The sprawled-out cities
Ever stretching further,
Growing, growing, growing.

This land set apart
By deep and mighty oceans;
A land of God's abundance
Brought to fruition by man's imagination,
By work and by faith.

We, the people, speak.
We speak of ourselves.
Yes, this country was founded
On liberty and freedom,
And right to worship God,
On the ideals of individual independence,
Tolerance and love,
And "the pursuit of happiness".

Many times we have strayed along the way,
Yet we have built well,
Slowly but surely a firm foundation.

Yes, we have faith we shall yet
        attain these ideals,
For we know deep within ourselves
God's guidance has led us through
To make our land a blessed place.

And ultimately we must know
That the "happiness" we have long pursued
Is deep within our hearts and souls,
God's gift to man's eternal being.

Nelia M. Dosser

I Pledge Allegiance...

Although the original "Pledge of Allegiance" was written in 1892, it was not until 1945 that Congress gave official sanction to the pledge.

The pledge was originally written by Francis Bellamy, a clergyman and editor.

Shortly after Bellamy joined the staff of *The Youth's Companion* the magazine launched a national celebration of Columbus Day . . . 1892 was the 400th Anniversary of the discovery of America. Bellamy assisted James B. Upham in planning a program for this special event.

"Every school in the land will have a flag raising!" declared Upham when talking about the national celebration of Columbus Day.

On Upham's suggestion *The Youth's Companion* assembled a committee and began to enlist the support of state superintendents of education, governors, congressmen and even the President. The result was a universal holiday declared by President Benjamin Harrison.

"Francis," said Mr. Upham, glowing with the success of the campaign, "I feel that the special day should mark a new consecration of patriotism. There should be some sort of an official program for universal use in all the schools."

Bellamy nodded. "The highlight of the program will be the raising of the flag. There should be a salute recited by the pupils in unison. "The 'Balch' salute which runs 'I give my heart and my hand to my country—one country, one language, one flag' seems lacking in dignity. It is my thinking that a vow of loyalty or allegiance to the flag should be the dominant idea."

"Allegiance . . . allegiance," repeated Upham. "That's the key word. Try writing the salute around that word, allegiance."

Later, when asked how he composed "The Pledge of Allegiance," Bellamy wrote:

"Beginning with the new word 'allegiance,' I first decided that 'pledge' was a better word than 'vow' or 'swear;' and that the first person singular should be used, and that 'my' flag was preferable to 'the.' When those first words, 'I pledge allegiance to my flag' looked up at me from the scratch paper, the start appeared promising. Then: should it be 'country,' 'nation,' or 'Republic?' Republic won because it distinguished the form of government chosen by the fathers and established by the Revolution. The true reason for allegiance to the flag is the 'Republic for which it stands.'

"Now how should the vista be widened so as to teach the national fundamentals? I laid down my pencil and tried to pass our history in review. It took in the sayings of Washington, the arguments of Hamilton, the Webster-Hayne debate, the speeches of Seward and Lincoln, the Civil War. After many attempts all that pictured struggle reduced itself to three words, 'ONE NATION, INDIVISIBLE.'

"But what of the present and future of this indivisible Nation? What were the old and fought-out issues which always will be issues to be fought for? Here was a temptation to repeat the historic slogan of the French Revolution, imported by Jefferson, 'liberty, equality, fraternity.' But that was rather quickly rejected as fraternity was too remote of realization, and equality was a dubious word. What doctrines, then, would everybody agree upon as the basis of Americanism? 'Liberty and Justice' were surely basic. If these were exercised 'for all' they involved the spirit of equality and fraternity. So that final line came with a cheering rush.

> "*'I pledge allegiance to my flag and (to) the Republic for which it stands—one Nation indivisible—with liberty and justice for all.'*
> *—Francis Bellamy, 1892*

"That, I remember, is how the sequence of the ideas grew and how the words were found. I called for Mr. Upham and repeated it to him.

"He liked it. His colleagues on *The Youth's Companion* also approved of it and it was printed in the official program.'"

Over the years the text of the Pledge of Allegiance underwent minor revisions. The words "my flag" were changed to "the flag of the United States" in 1923 at the first National Flag Conference and in 1924 the words "of America" were added to that phrase. In 1942 legislation was adopted by Congress to codify and emphasize existing customs pertaining to the display and use of the U.S. flag. The text of the pledge as written by Bellamy and modified by the National Flag Conference was inserted in this legislation, although the pledge itself was not designated as official.

In 1954, nine years after the "Pledge of Allegiance" was made official by Congress, President Dwight Eisenhower signed into law the bill inserting "under God." His signature was written on this bill on a most appropriate day. It was Flag Day.

Meanwhile, a controversy had developed over who had written the pledge. In 1923 the *Youth's Companion* organization denied Bellamy's authorship, saying it was a point of policy never to give credit for work done by editorial staff members.

Following Bellamy's death the family of the late James B. Upham made claim in Upham's name to the authorship of the pledge, a claim which Upham, himself, had not made. The matter was submitted in 1939 to a committee of three eminent historians named by the United States Flag Association.

After reviewing evidence presented by the families of both men, the committee decided that Bellamy was incontrovertibly the author, and in 1945 his authorship was recognized in the Congressional Record.

Evelyn Witter

GOLDEN NUGGETS

If we abide by the principles taught in the Bible, our country will . . . prosper. But if we and our posterity neglect the instructions and authority in this book, no man can tell how sudden a catastrophe may overtake us and bury our glory in profound obscurity.

Daniel Webster

Improvement

The Improvement of our way of life is more important than the spreading of it. If we make it satisfactory enough, it will spread automatically. If we do not, no strength of arms can permanently impose it.

Charles A. Lindbergh

"All That I Am"

Sink or Swim, live or die, survive or perish, I give my hand and my heart to this vote for the Declaration of Independence. . . . You and I may rue it. We may not live to the time when this Declaration shall be made good. We may die as Colonists, die as slaves, die ignominiously and on the scaffold! Be it so! If it be the pleasure of Heaven that my country shall require the poor offering of my life, this victim shall be ready. But while I do live, let me have a country, or at least the hope of a country, and that a free country. Before God, I believe the hour is come. My judgment approves this measure, and my whole heart is in it. All that I have, and all that I am, and all that I hope in this life, I am now ready here to stake upon this Declaration of Independence. It is my living sentiment, and by the blessing of God, it shall be my dying sentiment: Independence now, and Independence forever!

John Adams

The Liberty Bell

Liberty was a much-prized quality in the American Colonies long before the Declaration of Independence. The province of Pennsylvania had a liberal government and a policy of religious toleration which protected the rights of its citizens. It was no accident, then, that when Pennsylvania decided to order a bell in 1751, they asked that about its shoulder should be inscribed the 10th verse of the 25th chapter of Leviticus: "Proclaim liberty throughout all the land unto all the inhabitants thereof." The order was conveyed to Whitechapel Foundry, London, and in September 1752, the bell was landed ashore in America. Impatient to hear it ringing, the assemblymen ordered it set up in the State House yard and Philadelphians gathered round to hear its first sounds. It cracked, however, upon the first stroke.

Two local workmen undertook to recast it and succeeded at the second attempt.

Soon after the bell was suspended in its tower, it was used for summoning the people to the State House to receive important news.

For 23 years it summoned legislators to the Assembly in Philadelphia . . . The bell rang the Assembly together, February 3, 1757, when they directed Benjamin Franklin to "go home to England" to solicit redress of grievances . . . When the Stamp Act went into operation, October 31, 1765, the bell was muffled and tolled when the people mourned the "death of liberty" . . . The bell was rung September 27, 1770, to assemble the people, where they resolved that the claims of Parliament to tax the colonies were subversive of their constitutional rights . . . Following receipt of tidings of the Battle of Lexington, April 25, 1775, the bell called together 8000 people who assembled in the State House yard and agreed, unanimously, "to associate for the purpose of defending with arms, our lives, liberty, and property against all attempts to deprive us of them."

The historic second session of the Continental Congress was already underway and the resolution sponsored by Richard Henry Lee was presented June 7, 1776, declaring "that these United Colonies are, and of right ought to be, free and independent states, that they are absolved from all allegiance to the British Crown and that all political connection between them, and the State of Great Britain, is and ought to be totally dissolved." The Lee resolution was agreed to July 2, and the Declaration, penned by Thomas Jefferson after revision in committee, was adopted July 4.

The old State House Bell, as it was then called, was now to "Proclaim liberty throughout all the land unto all the inhabitants thereof," to ring out independence, to have its sequel taken up in every town and hamlet, to set in motion a never-ceasing force against tyranny and oppression.

John F. Cunningham

GOLDEN THOUGHT

I leave you, hoping that the lamp of liberty will burn in your bosoms, until there no longer be a doubt that all men are created free and equal.

Abraham Lincoln

Abraham Lincoln Pleads For Repentance

"Inasmuch as we know that by His divine law nations, like individuals, are subjected to punishments and chastisements in this world, may we not justly fear that the awful calamity of civil war which now desolates the land may be but a punishment inflicted upon us for our presumptuous sins to the needful end of our national reformation as a whole people?

"We have been the recipients of the choicest bounties of heaven; we have been preserved these many years in peace and prosperity; we have grown in number, wealth, and power as no other nation has ever grown. But we have forgotten God.

"We have forgotten the gracious Hand which preserved us in peace and multiplied and enriched and strengthened us, and we have vainly imagined, in the deceitfulness of our hearts, that all these blessings were produced by some superior wisdom and virtue of our own.

"Intoxicated with unbroken success, we have become too self-sufficient to feel the necessity of redeeming and preserving grace, too proud to pray to the God who made us. It behooves us, then, to humble ourselves before the offended Power, to confess our national sins, and to pray for clemency and forgiveness.

"Now, therefore, in compliance with the request, and fully concurring in the views of the Senate, I do by this my proclamation designate and set apart Thursday, the thirtieth day of April, 1863, as a day of national humiliation, to abstain on that day from their ordinary secular pursuits and to unite in their several places of public worship and devote to the humble discharge of the religious duties proper to that solemn occasion. All this being done in sincerity and truth, let us then rest humbly in the hope authorized by the divine teachings, that the united cry of the nation will be heard on high and answered with blessings no less than the pardon of our national sins and the restoration of our divided and suffering country to its former happy condition of unity and peace."

March 30, 1863

Let's Read It Together
the chilDReN's corNeR

Pepe

Joe was afraid to go home from school. In his pocket was a note from his teacher, probably telling about the fight he had started with his new friend, Johnny. He walked slowly, knowing Mama would be very angry with him.

He was glad he had started the fight, though. Johnny had called him "Pepe" and said his mother didn't talk right.

Mama was frying tortillas when he came in the kitchen door. She stopped long enough to give him a big hug and the milk and cookies that she always had ready for him.

"*Hola,* Pepe!" She greeted him.

He loved her so much, but he wished she would call him "Joe" and talk English like everyone else's mother. When Johnny came over, she called him "Juanito" and talked mostly in Spanish like she always did at home.

Mama read the note and smiled. "I must go to school with you tomorrow, Pepe," she told him. "We will talk together."

"I am sorry that I got into trouble, Mama," Joe tried to explain.

"What trouble, Pepe? Your teacher, Mrs. Swan, wants me to talk to her about helping with your class. She says nothing about trouble." Mama looked closely at the note.

"Oh, I got angry in school, but it wasn't trouble, I guess," Joe answered.

He wondered how Mama would help in school. Maybe she was needed to make cookies for a class party. He knew that he would have to fight some more. Mama would call him "Pepe," and she would call the other children by Spanish names and talk Spanish to them. Everyone would soon be making fun of the way his mama talked.

It was a short walk to school, and the children stared at Joe and his mother as they came into the classroom and hung their coats in the closet.

While everyone was busy with the reading workbooks, Joe could hear his mother and Mrs. Swan talking quietly in a corner of the room. They weren't looking at him, but Joe's face was getting hot and red.

Soon both Mama and Mrs. Swan walked to the front of the class.

Continued on page 88

Continued from page 87

"Children," Mrs. Swan began, "Mrs. Sanchez, Joe's mother, has offered to help me teach all of you a little Spanish each day. I have wanted to teach you a new language for a long time, but I needed help. Now, we are lucky to have a mother who is able to speak both English and Spanish. She will teach us some of the things she knows."

Then Joe's mama was laughing and talking to the class. Each child learned his name in Spanish, and "Pepe" seemed the easiest of all to say. The children had fun hearing the Spanish words and tried to say them. They all smiled warmly as they said *"Adios, Senora Sanchez,"* when Joe's mama left.

Joe was happy when Johnny wanted to play with him after school. He was especially happy when Johnny told him, "Your mom really is smart, Pepe."

He didn't even mind being called "Pepe."

Louise Barth

My Name Is America

I am a country . . .

but I am more than a country. I am nearly two hundred years old, but my mountains, forests, and rivers are ageless. Before I was a dream in the minds of mortal men, they were beautiful realities in the hands of a beneficent Creator.

I am a nation . . .

but I am more than a nation. I am a republic of fifty sovereign states, each with its own heritage and individual greatness, each a vital part of one indivisible whole—the United States of America.

I am a government . . .

but I am more than a government. I am a symbol of plenty, a model of representative government, a hallmark of freedom, justice, and independence to hundreds of millions throughout the world.

I am a melting pot . . .

but I am more than a melting pot. I am a haven for the oppressed, a living adventure in brotherhood, a community of compassion, and a dynamic example of liberty under law, opportunity with responsibility, and democracy through equality.

My name is America!

William Arthur Ward

Thanksgiving

thanks be unto God for his
unspeakable gift.

II Corinthians 9:15

Day Of Praise

For the preciousness of living
We give daily thanks to Thee,
For the beauty of the earth
And our immortality.

Refreshing rain and fragrant flowers
Warm rays from the sun,
Shadows soft and evening star
When the day is done.

Bird calls on the whispering wind
Their cheery notes so sweet,
All the bounties Thou dost give
Makes our lives replete.

Tender love for families
Friendships rich and true,
Bring to us sweet memories
And fill our hearts anew.

We give thanks for all our blessings
Lord of all to Thee we raise
Gratefulness for daily manna
On this Thanksgiving day of praise.

Raymond Henry Schreiner

Thanksgiving Time

We're thankful for our country
And the freedom we may share;
For choice and opportunity
And the beauty everywhere.
For all the gifts of nature,
The flowers, birds and trees;
For meadows, hills and valleys,
Each fresh and gentle breeze.

We're thankful for the snowflakes,
The sunshine and the showers;
For each day to work and play
And restful night-time hours.
The pleasant roads and beaches,
Each river, lake and stream;
The forests and the mountains
Where quiet reigns supreme.

For little towns and farmland
And cities rising tall,
For family, friends and helpers—
We're grateful for them all.
For field and orchard harvest
With bounty we may share,
For love and understanding
And home and warmth and care.

We're thankful for the little things
That make a better life,
For health and hope and happiness
And strength to deal with strife.
Let's not take this for granted
Till Thanksgiving Day is here
But always count our blessings
Throughout the entire year.

Harriet Whipple

Greatest Source Of Joy

America's great thanksgivings have fallen in her severest struggles. The Puritans, in their dire need and danger, were possessed of life's greatest source of joy—a thankful heart.

Thankful people are usually those who possess little. The folk in the little cottage . . . the slender income spent on simple things . . . the lamplight in the evening, the friendly warmth of the kitchen fire . . . these truly feel with thankful hearts the goodness and the warmth of life.

In the complexity of the present day many are orphaned from the stimulating source of gratitude. But in the harvest festival of Thanksgiving we may recapture something of its native spirit, and with it a sense of the reality and color and simple joy which belongs to everyone.

Charles E. Crews

Necessity For Thanksgiving

When the New England colonies were first planted, the settlers endured many privations and difficulties. Being piously disposed, they laid their distresses before God in frequent days of fasting and prayer. Constant meditation on such topics kept their minds gloomy and discontented, and made them disposed even to return to their fatherland, with all its persecutions.

At length, when it was again proposed to appoint a day of fasting and prayer, a plain, common-sense, old colonist rose in the meeting and remarked that he thought they had brooded long enough over their misfortunes, and that it seemed high time they should consider some of their mercies: That the colony was growing strong—the fields increasing in harvests; the rivers full of fish, and the woods of game; the air sweet; the climate salubrious; their wives obedient, and their children dutiful; and above all, that they possessed what they came for—full civil and religious liberty. And therefore, on the whole, he would amend their resolution for a fast and propose in its stead a day of thanksgiving!

His advice was taken, and from that day to this, whatever may have been the disastrous experience of New England, the old stock of the Puritans have ever found enough of good in their cup to warrant them in appointing this great annual festival.

Wadsworth

GOLDEN THOUGHT

You cannot hope to enjoy the Harvest
Without first laboring in the Field.

Author Unknown

November's Gold

Topaz gems of honey yellow,
Gold Chrysanthemums in bloom . . .
Make November seem more mellow . . .
Sun-like warmth in a wintry room.

Katherine Paxson

Autumn

Diaphanous the water lies beneath the blue unclouded
    skies
A bit of chill is in the air and color riots everywhere,
Where once the trees were dressed in green, the maples
    red and gold are seen,
Snow-white birches tall and bold are shedding coins
    of molten gold,
Along the shore, the berries blue are dressed in
    leaves of scarlet hue,
Beaver houses piled up high with twigs, the winter's
    food supply,
A symphony of sound and flight, the honking geese, a
    wondrous sight!
It's autumn, and the earth is dressed in brilliance,
    ere it takes its rest.

Edith Shubert

Counting Our Blessings

Grandpa Grittinger is as unique a personality as ever existed in a retirement home anywhere. Gramps and I don't always see eye to eye on how to raise children in the '70's. When Ralph and I were young, the depression was raging, and all that parents worried about was keeping their children alive till they reached eighteen.

But today, in this permissive age, Grandpa Grittinger takes a jaundiced view of our overadvantaged children. He sees Susan spend more for a coat than he earned in a whole week back in 1932. And as for a Thanksgiving table laden with sweet potatoes and gravy and spiced apples and mints and pies and ice cream, he wonders if anyone remembers when he sold apples at the corner of State and Madison in Chicago on Saturday afternoons.

Nonetheless, having Grandpa Grittinger at the head of the table on Thanksgiving is as traditional as the turkey itself, and this year Gramps arrived as usual in his 1958 Plymouth with his red vest and gold tie, and dinner began on schedule with the Doxology and a poem which Peter had composed at school.

It was not, however, a poem about thankfulness. It might be better described as "Ode to a Pumpkin Pie." And the children, in general, were not in one of their better moods. I had promised Jack and Peter the drumsticks, thinking Susan too old to care anymore, and she said she didn't want any of the dumb old bird at all.

Jack, meanwhile, declared that the chestnuts in the dressing ruined it, and when Peter discovered I'd made only mince pies this year and no pumpkin, he said it was a stupid Thanksgiving dinner.

Up till now, Grandpa Grittinger had borne it all silently. Up till now he had listened without comment to the grumbling and griping. But suddenly, at Peter's remark, he stood up, picked up the turkey platter in one hand and the sweet potatoes in the other.

"Well, if nobody's aware of the starving children in India," he said, "I'll just remove this turkey from the table." And he did. And before the children could close their astonished mouths, he was back for the cranberries and gravy. "And if nobody's grateful for the bounteous blessings which God has bestowed on us, I'll remove these too," he said, and disappeared. At this point I would have settled for a simple thank-you to the cook. But suddenly the children began to feel thankful, all right, and a moment later they were being grateful all over the place. Before he brought back the turkey, Grandpa Grittinger made each of them recite ten reasons why sitting at our Thanksgiving table was preferable to sitting on a sidewalk in Calcutta, and it was probably the most appreciated dinner I've ever made.

Phyllis Reynolds Naylor

This Day Is Autumn

MORNING:

When I awoke this morning
the mist was swirling around
our protruding mountain peaks,
but the foot hills were wrapped
in Oriental rugs.

NOON:

Now the wind has swept the mist away,
and the mountains display their white wigs.
Our bay is veiled either in soft gray fog
or sparkling with white sails.
When I went out to pick asters,
I realized . . . it is autumn. The goldenrod
proclaims the imminence of crisp days.

NIGHT:

The moonlight is using the willow leaves
to make autumn patterns on our quiet pond.

Nonee Nolan

The Maple Tree

Most of the trees stand naked now. The frost,
The wind, the rain have laid the bright leaves low.
The ginkos dropped their fans, expecting snow.
Cherry leaves strewed the ground like gold coins lost.
The dogwood's crimson flames are fallen now;
No trace of scarlet shows on any bough.
The oak still keeps its dry brown leaves rustling.
They will not fall until the buds of spring
Push them away, but one bright maple tree
Still flaunts its ocher leaves for all to see.
A splash of sunlight on the darkened day,
It brightens up the park and lights the way.
It will not shed its leaves until snow-fall
Clinging, weighs down the branches, covering all.

M. Albertina

Thanksgiving In Canada

In some respects, Thanksgiving in Canada is similar to the holiday in the United States. It is an autumn celebration which originated with a thanks offering by early New World settlers. It has become a harvest-related festival which is marked by bountiful dinners and large family reunions.

The Canadian Thanksgiving, however, is no mere imitation of the United States celebration, and its roots go back farther than many people realize. It is believed that the first formal Thanksgiving in the New World was celebrated in Canada in 1578—forty-two years before the Pilgrims landed in what was to become Massachusetts.

Sir Martin Frobisher was a British explorer who made several voyages to the New World during the sixteenth century. He was searching primarily for the Northwest Passage, but on one journey he found a sample of ore which he believed to be gold. Upon returning to England, he organized a gold-mining expedition which sailed to Newfoundland in 1578 in an attempt to found a permanent settlement.

It was here that the first American Thanksgiving was reportedly celebrated. Sir John Frobisher, brother of Sir Martin and co-organizer of the expedition, led the service, which offered thanks for the travelers' safe journey to the New World.

The ore which Frobisher had discovered was not really gold, and the settlement did not survive. In fact, no sixteenth-century attempt to establish an American colony turned out to be permanent. It was with this expedition, though, that the idea of celebrating Thanksgiving in the New World originated.

Thanksgiving did not become an annual autumn holiday in Canada until 1879. For many years the celebrations were held on the fourth Thursday in November, the day of the United States holiday. While attempts to change the date in the United States have never succeeded, the Canadian celebration went through a number of changes before a permanent date was established.

First, the day on which the holiday was celebrated was changed from a Thursday to a Monday. Canadian officials felt that it was necessary to provide more traveling time before this day of reunions, so Thanksgiving became the last day of a three-day weekend. After the end of World War I, the date was changed again. At that time the holiday was moved to Monday of the week of November 11th and became associated with Armistice Day festivities.

The final change came in 1931, when Canadians decided that a harvest festival in a land of early winters should not be held so late in the season. In that year they began celebrating Thanksgiving on the second Monday in October. This date apparently satisfies most Canadians because it has remained unchanged for forty-four years.

We Give Thanks

We have Freedom . . .

> God's richest gift
> And today
> The lingering hope
> Of the oppressed
> In other lands.
>
> For that Freedom
> We give Thanks.

We have Faith . . .

> In God
> In Nations
> In Man
> And in ourselves.
>
> For that Faith
> We give Thanks.

We have Hope . . .

> That all peoples
> Of God's world
> Will be united
> In everlasting Peace.
>
> For that Hope
> We give Thanks.

We have Courage . . .

> To defend the
> Cause of Freedom
> With our lives
> Our fortunes and
> Our sacred honor.
>
> For that Courage
> We give Thanks.

We have Memories . . .

> We do not forget
> American bravery
> And sacrifice at
> Valley Forge
> Tripoli
> The Alamo
> Gettysburg
> San Juan Hill
> The Argonne
> Normandy Beaches
> Iwo Jima
> Korea
> And Vietnam.
>
> For those Memories
> We give Thanks.

...he Pilgrims of 1621 . . . *they had so little* . . . Yet they
...ınd it in their hearts to give Thanks for what they had.
...We Americans of 1977 . . . *we have so much* . . . We,
...o, give Thanks for what *we* have.

We have the Bell . . .

> The Liberty Bell
> Whose inspiring
> Chimes now echo
> On foreign shores
> And whose
> Song of Freedom
> Is drowning out
> The bloody dirge
> Of communism.
>
> For that Bell
> We give Thanks.

We have Wisdom . . .

> To know that
> There are many
> Enemies *at home*
> Who seek
> Stealthily to
> Take our Freedoms
> From us,
> From our children
> And our children's
> Children.
>
> For that Wisdom
> We give Thanks.

We have Unity . . .

> Though we may
> Disagree
> Among ourselves,
> At any real threat
> To our Freedom
> A *united* America
> Rises in her might.
>
> For that Unity
> We give Thanks.

And so we pray:

> Give to us all
> The strength
> To *keep* Freedom
> At home . . .
> To spread Freedom
> Abroad . . .
> To pass Freedom
> On to the
> Next generation
> And to unborn
> Generations
> In a world
> At peace.

Robert Gordon Smith

We Thank Thee

For what shall we give thanks today?
　　Our Nation walks the peaceful way,
For glorious flag and liberty
　　Our country called "land of the free."
For field and plain and forest tree
　　Stretching on from sea to sea.
For Pilgrims, who brought not a sword
　　But in their hands the "Holy Word"
Who gave Thee thanks for gifts outpoured
　　For all of these we thank Thee, Lord.

For what shall we give thanks today?
　　For God, our Church, the right to pray,
For friends and homes, good food to eat,
　　God's blessings, making life so sweet,
For other things like sunshine bright
　　And all the stars that shine at night,
For health, and happiness, and strength
　　To meet the need of each day's length.
For guidance, care, thy "Living Word"
　　For all of these we thank Thee, Lord.

Edith Shubert

Thanksgiving Day

Why should Thanksgiving Day be only once a year? Let us make every day Thanksgiving Day. Thank God each morning for a wonderful day, for health and vitality of body, for knowledge to do our work well, for wisdom to follow the right path ourselves and to help others. Thank God each evening for His loving care and guidance during the day, for the abundance with which we are blessed and for sharing with others, for the beautiful things in the world . . . the flowers, the sunsets, music, beautiful scenery, interesting places and people, wonderful books which open the way to new vistas and new understandings. Thank God for loved ones and friends. Let us have Thanksgiving every day in the year!

Nelia M. Dosser

Thanksgiving

On other days of thanks I've said,
"Thank Thee, dear Lord, for this, my bread;
For clothing warm, for firelight's glow,
For loving friends—all these I know
Are things that make my life complete—
Good friends, a home, and food to eat;
And so I thank Thee, Lord."

Another year, with love-lit eyes,
I sang Thanksgiving to the skies;
"A lover's kiss, a promise made—
No finer riches would I trade
For this—for love's clear golden joy
In richness outshines earth's alloy—
And so I thank Thee, Lord."

A later year, with dreams come true—
A baby dear, with eyes of blue—
I humbly said, "For sending me
This miniature of Heaven, to Thee
A voice o'erfilled with thanks I raise
In heartfelt joy to sing Thy praise;
And so I thank Thee, Lord."

But now today my lips are still,
No words of praise pour forth to fill
The air with gratitude to Thee,
For all things I can feel and see;
My heart, instead, I open wide,
And for the deepened faith inside
I want to thank Thee, Lord.

For memories throughout the years,
For days of sunshine and of tears,
For constant love, for little things
That mean far more than wealth of kings;
For finding faith, and finding God
Was with me every path I trod,
I want to thank Thee, Lord . . .

Ruth Dallwig Campbell

Green Mountain Boys' Thanksgiving.

It was the late fall of 1769. The weather was cold, so frosty that there was a fringe of ice on Lake Wononscopomuc. The warmest place anywhere around the lake was the furnace at the lake's outlet, where they were running a charge of limestone, charcoal and ore from Ore Hill. One of the men at the furnace looked out and saw a spit of snow in the air and turned to another workman and said, "Old Ethan'll be along, if I know Ethan. Mark my word, he'll be along, to get one of those geese out there on the lake for his Thanksgiving dinner." And the other man, who was too young to remember when Ethan Allen was a partner in the furnace, along with the Forbes brothers, Samuel and Elisha, and Mr. Hazeltime, said, "It's too cold to get a goose." And the first man laughed. "You don't know Ethan. He's tough as rawhide and hard as pig-iron, and this is weather just to suit him. Besides, Ethan likes roast goose."

The man was right. Soon after noon Ethan Allen appeared, riding a big bay horse and carrying his long-barreled Pennsylvania rifle. He had ridden down from North Canaan, where he and Samuel Forbes were partners in a furnace and forge on the Blackberry River. He rode down to the forge there on Wononscopomuc and tied his mount to the hitching post and came in under shelter beside the furnace long enough to warm his hands. The man who had predicted his coming greeted him and asked, "You come to get a goose, Mr. Allen?" And Ethan nodded, then turned away.

Ethan walked along the shore, watching a flock of geese, and at last he lifted his long rifle and fired his shot. The geese took wing, all but the biggest goose of all, which fluttered once and floated, dead. And the men at the furnace watched as Ethan Allen stripped off his clothes and swam out and got his goose and swam back to shore and shook himself like a huge dog and put on his clothes again.

The men at the furnace were still staring, unbelieving, when Ethan returned, the goose over his shoulder. He didn't even come to the furnace to warm his hands. He tied the goose behind his saddle and was about to mount when the men at the fire walked out to him, and the older of the two touched his sleeve, just to be sure, and said, "Mr. Allen, when are you going to the Grants? I'd admire to go along. Mr. Allen, I'd even admire to die, if it happens. When are you going, tomorrow?"

"Tomorrow," Ethan said, "is Thanksgiving. I've got me a goose to eat tomorrow, and I intend to eat it." He got on his horse. "Come along," he said, "if you'd like to. You'll likely starve and freeze and die, up in the northern hills, but you'll die in glory." And he rode off, back toward North Canaan.

The two furnace workers watched him go, then went back and laid down their tools and followed him. And at every turn of the road they were joined by other men who had talked to Ethan.

They caught up with Ethan at an inn along the way. Ethan had stopped to warm himself. They joined him there. Day thinned to dusk and dusk became night, and bully-boys from all the furnaces and forges came to the inn, hearing that Ethan was there.

That was a night, as they say. When the sun came up on Thanksgiving Day Ethan Allen went out and brought in the goose and gave it to the cook, and the cook roasted it while Ethan got all his recruits on their feet and led them in a prayer of thanks for life and country and the cause of freedom. Then they ate. They ate roast goose till they could eat no more.

And the next day Ethan Allen started north, leaving a deserted inn behind him there at the foot of Smith Hill. Fifty men went with him, fifty of the toughest men in all Connecticut, but only the first of well over two hundred Connecticut Yankees Ethan rallied to fight the British. They were the Green Mountain Boys, of course, but they came out of the Connecticut hills. Ethan Allen recruited them here on Thanksgiving Day of 1769. Or so I have been told.

Hal Borland

Heap high the board with plenteous cheer,
    and gather to the feast,
And toast the sturdy Pilgrim band whose
    course never ceased.
Give praise to that All-Gracious One
    by whom their steps were led,
And thanks unto the harvest's Lord
    who sends our daily bread.

Alice Williams Brotherton

God's Goodness

Do you ever see God's goodness
In the brilliant setting sun?
In the laughter of small children?
In the stars when day is done?

In the gentle hand extended
During times of trial or care?
All are tokens of God's blessings,
They surround us everywhere.

As I pause to count my blessings
My heart o'erflows with love,
I'm so thankful for the goodness
Of my God who reigns above.

Elsie Leslie

Thanksgiving Prayers

It is revealing—and relaxing—to capture the feelings and reflections of children who haven't been exposed to the confusion of what we call World Affairs. One Thanksgiving a teacher asked her class to tell her what they, individually, would thank God for in their Thanksgiving prayer. After receiving all their replies, the teacher made the following composite into one prayer:
"We bow our heads and thank Thee—
—for the sound of laughter,
—for colored leaves that swirl and fall in the autumn,
—for the smell of chocolate cake in the oven,
—for big, red garden tomatoes,
—for my playful kitten that gets tangled up in pink yarn,
—for erasers that make mistakes disappear,
—for the feel of wet grass on my bare feet,
—for the good taste of hot cherry pie,
—for my warm, soft bed,
—for my sister's smile on Christmas morning,
—for the boats and sea gulls on the wallpaper that carry
    me across the sea when I look at them,
—for the shade of the maple trees in our yard,
—for windows that let me watch the world go by, and
—for God's care."

Fred B. Palmer

Polly's Thanksgiving List

Indian summer was over. On this November day in 1789 gray skies threatened New York City with a stormy Thanksgiving.

In Polly Simpson's schoolroom the children were telling their plans for the holiday. Polly brushed the soft brown hair away from her face and looked shyly at the other children. "We're going to eat turkey and pumpkin pie tomorrow. Jamie's never had Thanksgiving before."

She had already explained to her schoolmates about Jamie MacRae. He had lived in an orphanage in Baltimore and then with an uncle who had treated him badly. A week ago Polly's father had brought Jamie to stay with the Simpsons. He was 13, five years older than Polly, and was starting as an apprentice clerk in Mr. Simpson's warehouse.

"We're going to St. Paul's Chapel for the Thanksgiving service," added Polly. "President Washington will be there."

The teacher, Miss Ogilvie, picked up a printed news sheet from her desk. "That reminds me, children. I would like you to hear once again President Washington's message setting aside tomorrow, November 26, as a day for giving thanks."

New York was the capital of the country now, and each day on her way to school Polly passed by the Washingtons' house on Pearl Street. Once she had curtsied to the President as he was walking in Battery Park. She thought of George Washington as her friend, so she listened carefully to the message. Though she didn't understand all the long words, she knew that President Washington was asking the people to give thanks for God's care, for the beginning of the new United States, and for freedom to worship as they wished.

When the reading was finished, Miss Ogilvie said, "As your writing exercise today, each of you may set down the things you are thankful for."

Polly took her quill pen. With many blots and spatterings, she wrote: "I am thankful for my father and mother, for Tippy, our cat,

Continued on page 106

Continued from page 105

for my warm red mittens, and for food every day."

One more thing Polly was thankful for. But that was a secret. So she waited until lessons were over. Then she added a line at the bottom of her list, in large letters: "Thank thee, God, especially for Jamie, my brother." Perhaps Jamie wouldn't want to be her brother. But Polly had decided she wanted him. She folded the list and tucked it happily into the pocket of her school apron.

It was still there when she reached home after school. The kitchen smelled of spices and pastries cooking for the feast tomorrow.

"Polly, dear," said her mother, "step along the passageway and see to Jamie. He came from the warehouse an hour ago, looking white as suet."

"Is he sick?" asked Polly anxiously.

"Aye, sick at heart," Mrs. Simpson answered. "He spilled ink over two pages of the account book, and he's afraid of what will happen when it's discovered. I tried to tell him he wouldn't be punished, but, poor lad, he's had no chance to know kindness or mercy. We must help him realize he has a family now to love him."

Polly hung up her bonnet and shawl, damp from the rain that had begun falling. She started along the passageway to the little cubbyhole that had been her playroom until Jamie arrived. Before she reached the door, a tall, dark-eyed boy in knee breeches and broadcloth coat stepped out. He carried a bundle tied in a kerchief.

"Jamie, what are you doing? Are you running away?"

Jamie looked at her fiercely. "Why not? I never should have come in the first place. I put you out of your room. I've made extra work for your mother. I'm so fumble-fingered. I spoiled a morning's accounts at the warehouse."

"But you can't leave!" exclaimed Polly. "You're going to be my brother." There, the secret was out. Whether it made Jamie angry or not, she had to tell him; she had to make him understand that he belonged here. "Father said you are one of the family. That means you're my brother. Please stay."

The fierceness left Jamie's face. His dark eyes were bewildered. Still he couldn't believe her. Polly plucked the paper from her apron pocket and pushed it into his hand. In the dim light of the passageway Jamie unfolded the Thanksgiving list. He read it slowly, whispering the last words, "especially for Jamie, my brother." Then he set down his bundle and caught Polly in a tremendous hug.

The storm on Thanksgiving Day, 1789, kept many good citizens away from the service at St. Paul's Chapel. But President Washington was in his pew, and behind him sat the Simpsons, Polly next to Jamie. They all had much for which to be thankful.

Dorothy Ballard

Friendship

GREATER LOVE HATH NO MAN THAN THIS, THAT
A MAN LAY DOWN HIS LIFE FOR HIS FRIENDS.

JOHN 15:13

Tell Him So

If you have a word of cheer
That may light the pathway drear,
Of a brother pilgrim here,
   Let him know.
Show him you appreciate
What he does, and do not wait
Till the heavy hand of fate
   Lays him low.
If your heart contains a thought
That will brighter make his lot,
Then, in mercy, hide it not;
   Tell him so.

Wait not till your friend is dead
Ere your compliments are said;
For the spirit that has fled,
   If it know,
Does not need to speed it on
Our poor praise; where it has gone
Love's eternal, golden dawn
   Is aglow.
But unto our brother here
That poor praise is very dear;
If you've any word of cheer,
   Tell him so.

F. A. Egerton

Friendship

Friendship needs no studied phrases,
  Polished face, or winning wiles;
Friendship deals no lavish praises,
  Friendship dons no surface smiles.

Friendship follows Nature's diction,
  Shuns the blandishments of Art,
Boldly severs truth from fiction,
  Speaks the language of the heart.

Friendship favors no condition,
  Scorns a narrow-minded creed,
Lovingly fulfills its mission,
  Be it word or be it deed.

Friendship cheers the faint and weary,
  Makes the timid spirit brave,
Warns the erring, lights the dreary,
  Smooths the passage to the grave.

Author Unknown

GOLDEN THOUGHT

An old friend is like a full-blown rose, each velvet petal a pleasant memory. Its fragrance recalls sweetness that grows with years of love, understanding, and sympathy.

Margaret Crawford

Biography Of A Rose

I picked my first flower yesterday,
A rosebud kissed with dew
And passed its flawless beauty on
To someone sad I knew.

She thanked me with her shy sweet smile
Then gave the rose away.
For it was all she had, she said,
And it was Father's Day.

At eventide it traveled on
Where someone tossed in pain,
Then kind hands cut the thorns away
And passed it on again.

Today my rose came back to me,
Clutched in a toddler's hand,
A broken, wilted gift of love,
Atop a cake of sand!

Louise Justice

Rescue In The Gorge

Tyler Seal and Rick Yoder decided to take a weekend hiking trip in Yosemite National Park. They started off July 7, a Saturday, and followed mapped trails for ten miles to a site called Ten Lakes. Here they did some climbing, cooked over a campfire, swam and fished.

On Sunday morning, they agreed that it would be more interesting to return by a different route. They went off-trail to make a one-mile descent to the Tuolumne River, which they intended to follow for two miles before picking up another mapped trail.

For five hours they cautiously worked their way around waterfalls, fallen trees, huge boulders and underbrush. By the time they reached the rushing, rock-strewn river, Tyler had fallen a few times. The river had no real bank, just a narrow, uneven rock ledging which they carefully walked along for about a mile. Then, at a bend in the river, the ledging dwindled and became sheer granite wall.

By now exhausted and apprehensive, they stared at the impasse. "There's a pool of shallow water down there," Rick said. "I'll jump in with a rope, so you can haul me back up. Maybe I'll be able to see something around the bend."

Tyler wound one end of the rope around his hand. Rick leaped eight feet into the river. As he started wading, his foot slipped on a rock. Fearing that he would pull Tyler in, he let go of the rope.

The gushing waters grabbed him and hurled him downstream. He tumbled through the white, roiling chute, caroming off rocks and frantically flailing his arms and legs to get his head above water. He surfaced, banged into a rock, grabbed it and held.

Back on the ledge, Tyler watched in horror as Rick vanished. He thought, *I might as well see if I can help,* and jumped in. He landed on a rock, breaking his left ankle. The water whirled him under. Then he hit a projecting rock, and the strength of the current miraculously lifted him on top of it. "Rick! Rick!" Tyler yelled.

"Tyler, I can't hold on!"

"Get on top of your rock!"

Rick somehow twisted his body. The current hit him broadside, lifting him, enabling him to scratch his way onto the rock. He lay there, half-gasping, half-sobbing, and looked around. Tyler's rock was in the middle of the river, but Rick's was only eight or nine feet from the gorge wall. And, halfway to the wall, another rock jutted from the water. A leap to that rock, then to a wall ledge, and he would be out. "Stay there!" Rick shouted to Tyler. "I'm going for help."

Rick reached the gorge wall and began climbing. It was slow and torturous. Sometimes he found himself totally blocked and had to retreat. He knew that if he slipped he would drop into the river.

After some 300 yards, the side of the gorge grew less steep. He grimly continued his climb, pushing through thick brush, crawling between enormous boulders, climbing trees to get over small cliffs. The river was far below him, a thin white line in the fading light.

At nightfall he slumped down into a patch of weeds. He had to stop. He couldn't take a chance on falling in the darkness. It grew cold, and he shivered in his thin T-shirt.

Tyler was also shivering on his three-by-four-foot rock. He tried to find relief from the cold spray of the roaring river by pulling his T-shirt over his head. He prayed: *Please, God, help me. And help Rick. Don't let him fall. Give him strength to make it.*

Daylight offered no relief. The river, the rocks, the great canyon walls seemed indifferent to his terrible plight. He sang songs, repeated jokes, called out the names of the states. Nothing helped.

He looked at his watch. It was 4:30 in the afternoon. If no help came by dawn, he would slip off the rock and try to make it to the gorge wall. He had no way of knowing that a waterfall, which would surely batter him to death, was just around the bend.

High above Tyler—and now miles away—an exhausted Rick had arrived at the ranger station where Pete Thompson and Richard Smith were on duty.

It was 5 p.m. The rangers immediately called for a civilian helicopter. By 6:15, Rick and Ranger Smith made the first pass over the gorge. They saw nothing. Tyler heard the machine, but assumed that his mind was playing tricks. He didn't look up.

The chopper made a second pass. This time Tyler saw it and waved. Rick spotted him and tapped Smith. "There he is!" he yelled.

After the chopper had landed in an open area near the top of the gorge, Smith radioed Tyler's position and predicament to Thompson. They agreed that Rick and Smith should climb down into the gorge and spend the night near Tyler to bolster his morale. Meanwhile, Thompson would ask the Navy if it could send a rescue helicopter.

With Rick acting as anchor man on the ropes, Smith eased himself down the gorge wall to within 45 feet of Tyler. "Can you make it another night?" the ranger called. "We'll have a helicopter with a cable here in the morning."

"I think I can."

"Angel 4" dipped into Yosemite Valley early the next morning to pick up Pete Thompson. The ranger quickly briefed the crew on the problem, emphasizing that every minute was precious because of steadily increasing wind velocity.

Pilot Morse made one pass over the gorge, then another pass through the gorge at about 400 feet. He quickly weighed all the factors that would affect the operation. Because every extra pound sub-

Continued on page 114

Continued from page 113

tracted from flying stability, Ranger Thompson was off-loaded on a little plateau about 1800 feet from Tyler Seal. "Okay," Morse announced finally. "We're going in."

As the helicopter sank into the gorge, each man assumed specific responsibilities. Pilot Morse played the craft's controls against the winds, and kept an eye on the south wall. Co-pilot Griesbach visually measured the distance between the rotor blades and the north wall, and at the same time scanned instruments and gauges. Chavers put on his harness and stuffed a second harness into his pocket. Jones reported the movements of the ship's tail.

Crew chief Hart, flat on his belly, directed Morse to a position 75 feet above the stranded hiker. "Forward," he said into his helmet mike. "Ten yards at 12 o'clock . . . easy forward . . . a little more to the left." Morse inched closer to the north wall.

"Easy . . . easy . . . HOLD! You're right on the money."

Hart used an electrically controlled winch to lower Chavers. "He's half way down . . . you're drifting . . . easy forward and left . . . HOLD! He's three quarters down . . . he's turning . . . he's there!"

Chavers settled on the rock as the thundering river raged by. "You all right?" he asked Tyler.

"Just my ankle."

"You'll be out of here in a couple of minutes."

Hart kept Morse informed of what was happening. "The kid is buckled . . . the cable is about to pick up the weight—NOW!"

Morse had to compensate for the additional weight of some 185 pounds imposed on one side of the ship. Hart moved the winch lever to its top speed. "He's halfway . . . three quarters . . . he's in!"

Morse said, "The wind is getting stronger." Hart got the message: the pilot was hovering a scant 12 feet from the granite wall; with the rising wind, only a few minutes remained before he would have to pull away from Chavers' position.

The crew chief dropped the cable. He swung the cable three times, getting the feel of the weight, then dropped the hook right into Chavers' hands. Chavers hooked up, Hart winched up, and Morse pulled away from the wall while Chavers was still swinging in the air. The entire rescue operation had taken just ten minutes.

Morse picked up Rangers Thompson and Smith and Rick Yoder. As the copter lifted away, Tyler gave Rick a big grin. "Thanks, buddy," he said, and promptly fell asleep.

Morse was proud of his crew. He also was relieved and exhausted.

Tyler Seal will never lose his awe of what happened. "I was a stranger to those men," he says. "To think that they knowingly risked their lives to save me. Maybe someday I'll understand what makes human beings want to do such things for other human beings."

Joseph P. Blank

Friends Old and New

Here's to the old friends true
Who share in all we do
And have learned all our ways
Through many yesterdays.
Theirs are the hearts that share
All that we meet of care;
Theirs are the eyes that see,
Though grave our faults may be,
The good that lies below.
That's why we love them so!

But here's to the happy day
When comes across our way
A new friend, blithe and bold,
To join the faithful old.
Glad is the sheltering door
To welcome in one more.
Brighter the fireplace where
We draw another chair,
But happiest, at day's end,
Are we to gain a friend.

Author Unknown

I Have A Friend

I have a friend! A friend who is true!
A friend I can tell every sorrow to.
I have a friend who stands by my side.
A friend to whom all things I confide.
I have a friend—one beyond compare!
Oh, World, a loyal friend is rare.
I have a friend who passed the test.
I have a friend!—I am truly blessed!

Frances Angermayer

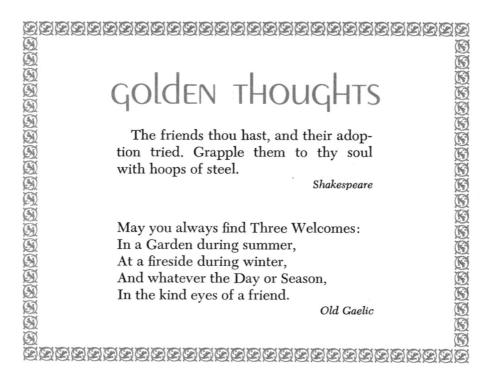

GOLDEN THOUGHTS

The friends thou hast, and their adoption tried. Grapple them to thy soul with hoops of steel.

Shakespeare

May you always find Three Welcomes:
In a Garden during summer,
At a fireside during winter,
And whatever the Day or Season,
In the kind eyes of a friend.

Old Gaelic

Snowball Kindness

Once, when approached by a friend who found himself in a financial jam and sought help, Franklin wrote: "I do not pretend to *give* you the sum you asked. I am only lending it to you. . . . When you meet with another honest man in similar distress, you must pay me by lending this sum to him, enjoining him to discharge his debt by a like operation when he shall be able and shall meet with another such opportunity. I hope it thus may go through many hands before it meets with a knave that will stop its progress. This is a trick of mine for doing a great deal of good with little money."

Author Unknown

The Gift Of Friendship

FRIENDSHIP is a PRICELESS GIFT
that cannot be bought or sold,
But its value is far greater
than a mountain made of gold —
For gold is cold and lifeless,
it can neither see nor hear,
And in the time of trouble
it is powerless to cheer —
It has no ears to listen,
no heart to understand,
It cannot bring you comfort
or reach out a helping hand —
So when you ask God for a GIFT,
be thankful if HE sends
Not diamonds, pearls or riches,
but the love of real true friends.

Helen Steiner Rice

The Kindly Neighbor

I have a kindly neighbor, one who stands
Beside my gate and chats with me awhile.
Gives me the glory of his radiant smile
And comes at times to help with willing hands.
No station high or rank this man commands;
He, too, must trudge, as I, the long day's mile;
And yet, devoid of pomp or gaudy style,
He has a worth exceeding stocks or lands.

To him I go when sorrow's at my door;
On him I lean when burdens come my way;
Together oft we talk our trials o'er,
And there is warmth in each good night we say.
A kindly neighbor! Wars and strife shall end
When man has made the man next door his friend.

Edgar A. Guest

GOLDEN NUGGET

Honest men esteem and value nothing
so much in this world as a real friend.
Such a one is as it were another self, to
whom we impart our most secret
thoughts, who partakes of our joy, and
comforts us in our affliction; add to this,
that his company is an everlasting pleasure to us.

Pilpay

An Old Story

Strange that I did not know him then,
    That friend of mine.
I did not even show him then
    One friendly sign;

But cursed him for the ways he had
    To make me see
My envy of the praise he had
    For praising me.

I would have rid the earth of him
    Once, in my pride.
I never knew the worth of him
    Until he died.

Edwin Arlington Robinson

Friends And Friendship

A little more kindness, A little less creed,
A little more giving, A little less greed,
A little more smile, A little less frown,
A little less kicking, A man when he's down,
A little more "we," A little less "I,"
A little more laugh, A little less cry,
A little more flowers, On the pathway of life,
And fewer on graves, At the end of the strife.

Anonymous

The Wall

Something there is that doesn't love a wall,
That sends the frozen-ground-swell under it,
And spills the upper boulders in the sun;
And makes gaps even two can pass abreast.

Before I built a wall, I'd ask to know
What I was walling in or walling out,

And to whom I was like to give offense.
Something there is that doesn't love a wall,
That wants it down!

Robert Frost

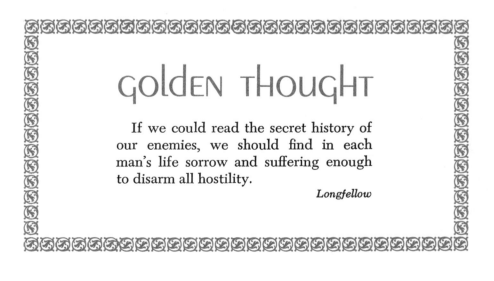

golden thought

If we could read the secret history of
our enemies, we should find in each
man's life sorrow and suffering enough
to disarm all hostility.

Longfellow

GOLDEN SCRIPTURE

Like A Shepherd

"He will feed his flock like a shepherd,
he will gather the lambs in his arms,
he will carry them in his bosom,
and gently lead those that are with young."

Isaiah 40:11

My Wealth

I have a wealth of patience;
      I have tolerance, and more,
I know that happiness is part
      Of my abundant store!
I have contentment also
      And love, a large amount.
And dividends of happiness
      Too great, for strict account.
I have the appreciation
      Of friends, for whom I care.
And so my wealth's unlimited —
      It comes from everywhere!

Velta Myrle Allen

Atonement

How often we neglect a friend
    When living—but should death appear,
The penitent heart is quick to send
    A wreath to lay upon his bier.

Margaret E. Bruner

golden thought

The world is not a lonely place. There is light and life and love enough for all of us. And I ask you, and all Americans, to reach out to join hands with me—and together we will seek it out.

Gerald Ford

Fulfillment

Lo, I have opened unto you the
    gates of my being,
And like a tide, you have flowed
    into me.
The innermost recesses of my spirit
    are full of you
And all the channels of my soul
    are grown sweet with your presence
For you have brought me peace;
    The peace of great tranquil waters,
And the quiet of the summer sea.
    Your hands are filled with peace as
The noon-tide is filled with light;
    About your head is bound the eternal
Quiet of the stars, and in your heart
    dwells the calm miracle of twilight.

I am utterly content.

Author Unknown

An Old Spanish Custom

Jim rolled his lawn mower and his old dilapidated bicycle into the tool shed and hurried to the house. He was going to be late again for ball practice if he didn't move fast. As he came through the door, his mother called from the kitchen, "Mike phoned a few minutes ago. He said he'd meet you at the usual corner around four o'clock."

"Thanks, Mom. I'm on my way," Jim called back. He grabbed his catcher's mitt and the door slammed behind him.

Mike was waiting. "Late again!" he greeted as Jim turned the corner. "Let's take the shortcut through the woods and save time. If you wouldn't mow so many lawns. . . ."

"I wouldn't be late so much," Jim finished, laughing. "But neither would I have a new bicycle by the time school starts this fall."

Suddenly Mike's attention was elsewhere. "Look, Jim. There's an old bus somebody has dumped right here on the edge of town."

Jim stopped. "That's not a bus. That's an old truck with a canvas top."

A woman lifted the rear flap and peered out. A small child tugged at her skirts. When she saw them, she quickly closed the canvas.

"Just a family of transients, I suspect, camping overnight," Mike suggested.

"Yeah. A lot of them go through about this time of year headed for one kind of crop or another," Jim added.

The boys got a ride home after ball practice and the old truck was, for the moment at least, forgotten.

Almost a week passed before Jim and Mike took the shortcut again. Surprise registered on their faces when they saw the truck still parked where they had first seen it.

As they came near, a boy who looked to be about their age walked from behind the truck. "Hello," Jim called. The boy looked startled. "I'm Jim Blake and this is Mike Davis," Jim said in a friendly voice.

The boy's dark features relaxed. "My name is Juan Martinez."

"Are you camping here for a while?" Mike asked.

"Only until my father can earn enough money to buy tires for the truck," Juan answered.

Jim and Mike came closer and looked at four tires—very flat and very full of holes. "Your father found work in town?" Jim asked, knowing how most of the townspeople felt about transients.

"My father can fix anything. They are letting him try out at the Fix-It Shop. He will show them!" Juan called proudly as Mike and Jim walked away.

Jim kept thinking of Juan and the old truck with the worn-out tires. "Let's take the shortcut," he said several days later. Secretly he hoped the truck and its occupants would be gone. Then he could forget them. But he was to be disappointed, for as he and Mike turned the last corner, there was the truck.

"Hello, Juan," Jim called loudly as he and Mike came closer. The woman came to the open end of the truck. The young child was in her arms. "Juan is in town looking for work," she said. Jim thought her face looked old and tired. Her eyes followed his to the tires. "Most of the money went for Maria's medicine. She has been very ill." The child began to whimper. "Juan is looking for yards to mow," the mother continued. "He is very good at mowing."

"Here he comes now," Jim announced. Juan did not look up as he approached.

"He found no work," the woman muttered and turned away.

"All the yards are promised," Juan said, his eyes still on the ground.

Jim felt a stab of guilt. He and several of his friends had pretty well tied up the lawnmowing business all over the small town.

Inside the hot truck, the child continued to fret.

Suddenly Jim felt that he must get away from this place. These people with their sadness and their great need gave him the "willies." He beckoned to Mike and with barely a "so long," they were gone.

Neither boy spoke for several minutes. It was Jim who broke the silence. "You go on home, Mike. I have some business with Juan."

"You need that new bike, Jim," Mike said.

Jim turned and hurried back to the truck. Juan looked surprised but said nothing. Jim was quiet for a moment, too. He could see a beautiful blue and silver English Racer rolling out of his reach. "Juan," he said quickly, "I mow many lawns. I was just wondering if you would help me out for a while."

Juan's black eyes grew round. "Si, si. Gracias, gracias!" he exclaimed, momentarily forgetting his English.

The next few weeks passed quickly. Only occasionally did Jim regret his generosity. "I'll give myself a new bike for Christmas," he replied jokingly to one of Mike's frequent reminders of what a soft heart had cost him.

Then one day when Jim came home from enrolling in junior high for the fall semester, his mother handed him a note. Scrawled on an

Continued on page 124

Continued from page 123

old newspaper wrapper, and written in a mixture of languages, Jim read: "Adios, bueno amigo. Your mower is inside the shed. A surprise is there, too. I hope you like it. Muchas gracias, Juan."

So they are gone, Jim thought on his way to the tool shed. And what surprise could Juan possibly afford? But when he opened the door, he knew. There stood his old bike, shining and beautiful in its new coat of blue and silver. He gave it a shake. It was positively sturdier than ever. Suddenly he remembered Juan's words that first day, "My father can fix anything."

Jim's mother followed him to the shed. "Juan found out about your bike problem and told his father. I tried to pay, but Mr. Martinez seemed almost insulted. 'My people return the kindness they receive,' he said proudly. 'It's an old Spanish custom.' "

Jim rubbed his hand over the bicycle. It felt like the touch of a good and trusted friend.

As he stepped outside, a first star peeped from behind a cloud. Jim remembered a custom of his own and made a wish. This time the wish was not for himself. It was for four people on their way to somewhere in an old truck with a canvas top.

Ann Hudson Downs

Because You Talked To Me

When I was so in need
Somehow you chanced to call
And you just talked to me
And I felt ten feet tall.
You didn't know my need
Nor could you ever see
The miracle wrought that day
When you just talked to me.
But friend, I felt so brave
When you left me that day
Because you talked to me
And knew just what to say.

Perry Tanksley

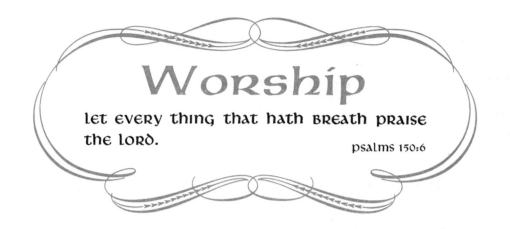

Worship

let every thing that hath breath praise the lord.

psalms 150:6

God Was There

I woke at glorious dawn
When happy bird-song filled the air—
    And God was there.

A wayside rose all wet with dew
Blossomed in perfumed beauty rare—
    And God was there.

The sunlight shimmered through the rain
And formed a rainbow to declare
    That God was there.

A mother soothed her fretful child
With tenderness beyond compare—
    And God was there.

All through a busy day I saw
Hope rise in triumph from despair—
    For God was there.

A precious little child was born
Into a home with love made fair—
    And God was there.

Life's candle flickered and went out
For one alone. Did someone care?
    Yes, God was there.

At twilight hush, with folded hands
I knelt in humble prayer—
    And God was there!

Sibyl A. Cox

GOldEN THOUGHT

There is but one God about whom
the universe performs perfectly.

Miriam Woolfolk

What Do You Stand To Lose?

Many years ago (long before the Communistic regime) this story
came out of Russia.

It seems that a certain atheist was parading up and down the
countryside, pouring out his verbiage against the very thought of
God, and ridiculing all those who believed in God.

On one occasion he addressed a group gathered in a large hall. He
stirred them to a high pitch, and then he hurled an invitation to God,
that if there be a God, He reveal it by smiting him to death. Of
course, God did not, and so he turned to his audience and said, "See,
there is no God."

Whereupon, a little Russian peasant woman with a shawl about her
head arose to speak. She addressed her remarks to the speaker and
said, "Sir, I cannot answer your arguments; your wisdom is beyond me.
You are an educated man; I am merely a peasant woman. With your
superior intelligence will you answer me one question?

"I have been a believer in Christ for many years. I have rejoiced in
His salvation, and I have enjoyed my Bible. His comfort has been a
tremendous joy. If, when I die, I come to learn that there is no God;
that Jesus is not the Son of God; that the Bible is not true; and there
is no salvation nor heaven, pray, sir, what have I lost by believing in
Christ during this life?"

The room was still. The audience grasped the woman's logic, and
then they turned to the atheist, who by that time was swayed by the
woman's simplicity. In quiet tones he remarked, "Madam, you won't
stand to lose a thing."

At which the peasant woman answered, "You have been kind and
answered my question. Permit me to ask another. If, when it comes
your time to die, you discover that the Bible is true, that there is a
God; that Jesus is His Son, and that there is a heaven and a hell; pray,
sir, what will you stand to lose?"

Of course, the logic was so overwhelming that the crowd leaped to
its feet and shouted in ecstacy.

Author Unknown

Faith

His conception
I believe that my Saviour's conception was pure,
That His Father was God up above,
That His coming from glory will ever endure
As a message of infinite love.

His birth
I believe that my Saviour was born of a maid
Who was truly a virgin in fact,
Who, though troubled in spirit, would not be afraid
Of this strange, and yet sanctified, act.

His life
I believe that my Saviour was true to His call
To exemplify God upon earth,
Though rejected so cruelly, to offer to all
His forgiveness, His healing, His worth.

His death
I believe that my Saviour was totally dead,
That He rested three days in the grave,
That He hung on the cross, that He suffered and bled,
That His blood is sufficient to save.

His resurrection
I believe that my Saviour arose from the tomb,
That He finished His work, as He said,
That He overcame death, with its terror and gloom,
That He offers us glory instead.

His ascension
I believe that my Saviour ascended on high,
Just as swift as a bird, and as free,
And that somewhere, with God, out beyond the blue sky,
He's preparing a mansion for me.

His return
I believe that my Saviour will honor His word,
For He said He was coming again,
That the sound of the trumpet will, one day, be heard.
And I thrill as I listen. Amen!

Alvy E. Ford

Faith Is A Star

And He said, "What is faith to you?" and I replied:

The road is dark,
The mist hangs low,
No moon above,
No light below.
I feel the blackness closing in,
And fear replaces peace within.
I cry aloud for help afar.
Despairing hands rend through the bar of clouds,
        And lo!
He's hung a shining star!

The world has turned its back on me,
There is no help that I can see;
But fog has changed
To brighter hue,
And when the sun breaks through the blue,
Behold! The face of God shines through!

Ruby A. Jones

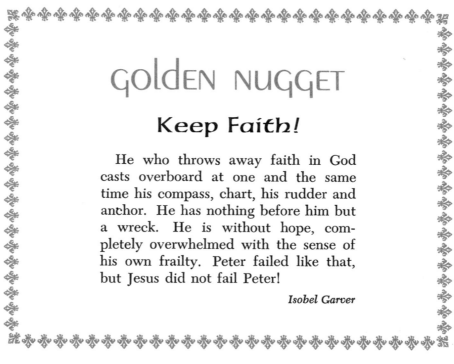

GOLDEN NUGGET

Keep Faith!

He who throws away faith in God casts overboard at one and the same time his compass, chart, his rudder and anchor. He has nothing before him but a wreck. He is without hope, completely overwhelmed with the sense of his own frailty. Peter failed like that, but Jesus did not fail Peter!

Isobel Garver

One Prayer

One candle, all alone,
sheds very little light;

one by one we add some others,
then the room is bright.

One prayer, all alone,
seems extremely weak;

we add some others, then,
we reach the Heart we seek.

Eleanor Di Giulio

Growing In Prayer

Freshly bathed, warm and drowsy in pink flannel, five-year-old Becky climbed into bed. "I'm not going to pray tonight," she told her mother. "There's nothing I want."

What do we want of God when we pray?

Young people want to get rid of skin blemishes or to pass their driver's tests. Older people want to lose weight or to stretch the paycheck another week.

Prayer is not a let-God-do-it substitute for action on our part. Perhaps the SOS we tap out to God could be solved by our own efforts.

A mother pulls on her child's stockings and shoes when the baby girl is 15 months old. How sad if she does so when the girl is 15 years old! The healthy young lady dresses herself.

How equally sad if we beg God to help us do something while we ourselves are not prepared to resolve the problem. And how very sad if all our prayers are of the 'gimme' variety. It has been said that most prayers could be answered either by a gift of money or by a kind friend. Asking is right, but it is good to think twice about our wants. What do we really want of God?

The disciples said to Jesus, 'Lord, teach us to pray' (Luke 11:1).

Catharine Brandt

When Father Prays

When father prays he doesn't use
    The words the preacher does.
They're different things for different
    days—
    But mostly it's for us.

When father prays the house is
    still—
    His voice is low and deep;
We shut our eyes, the clock ticks
     loud—
    So quiet we must keep!

He prays that we may be good boys,
    And later on good men;
And then we squirm and think we
     won't
    Have any quarrels again.

You'd never think to look at Dad
    He once had tempers too;
I guess if father needs to pray
    We youngsters surely do.

Sometimes the prayer gets very long
    And hard to understand;
And then I wiggle up quite close,
    And let him hold my hand.

I can't remember all of it,
    I'm little yet, you see;
But one thing I cannot forget—
    My father prays for me.

Author Unknown

Listen

Listen to the Voices of the Earth,
    And hear a Song of Praise—
Listen to the Wind,
    And hear a Symphony of Peace—
Listen to the Rain,
    And hear a Lullaby—
Listen to a Sunbeam,
    And hear the Harps of Heaven—
Listen to the Stars,
    And hear the Song of Angels—
Listen to a Rainbow,
    And hear the Promise of Tomorrow—

Listen, Listen—
And hear the most beautiful Sound there is,
    The Voice of Our Lord, Jesus Christ, the Son of God,
        Saying—
"In my Father's house are many mansions: if it were not so,
    I would have told you. I go to prepare a place for you.
And if I go and prepare a place for you, I will come again,
    and receive you unto Myself; that where I am, there
    ye may be also."

John 14:2, 3

Florence H. Cottrill

Footsteps

When I was a child, my sister and I walked along a country road about half a mile to school. When there was deep snow, my father walked before us, leaving his footprints for us to step into. He was conscious of our short strides and walked accordingly.

Jesus walked on earth, leaving "footsteps" for us to follow. He made allowances for our human frailties, yet He expected great things of His followers. We may not always want to go where His steps lead because we are lured into seemingly more interesting paths by the glitter of transient pleasures. Peter reminds us that those who follow Him will never walk in darkness. What a glorious prospect!

Ruth H. Short

golden scripture

Don't worry about anything; instead, pray about
everything; tell God your needs and don't forget
to thank him for his answers. If you do this you
will experience God's peace, which is far more
wonderful than the human mind can understand.
His peace will keep your thoughts and your hearts
quiet and at rest as you trust in Christ Jesus.

Philippians 4:6-7 (LB)

Let The Special Ones Come

Rita was ageless. She might have been 18 or 48, but her mind was
forever fixed at age four, and that had left its stamp on her bland,
wrinkle-free face.

One Sunday morning she brought another "big-little" friend to
church who lived with her in one of "those" homes. Over a thousand
worshipers had assembled, and the service had already started as they
commenced their naive procession, ambling down the center aisle to
the front where they finally found two vacant seats directly ahead
of me.

Eight people stood to let them struggle past to the empty seats in
the middle of the row. As Rita was about to sit down, the pastor
glanced toward the commotion and her eye caught his; her face
flooded with joy, and she waved a delighted gesture toward him.
Silently her lips formed the word "Hi!" and he nodded slightly and
smiled back. He had welcomed her openly in this large congregation,
and I loved him for it.

Though their faces registered no response, Rita and her friend sat
unobtrusive and quiet. During the singing of hymns, she showed her
friend how to hold one half of the hymnal. Garbling words of their
own making, they joined in singing each song in their own happy
way. Then the offering plate started down the row. What would
Rita give? I wondered. With a dowager's dignity, her purse clicked
open and she placed a nugget of gold for God in the plate—a shining
new penny.

gOLdEN VERSE

With The Dawn

With the dawn comes inspiration,
With the dawn hope springs anew;
God is in His fair Creation,
From earth's deep to Heaven's blue!

Helen Donaldson

I didn't understand when, during the Scripture reading, Rita turned around and whispered something unintelligible to me while pointing with one of her hands to a small Bible dangling open in the other. So I pointed to the Bible in my lap to show her I already had mine. She turned around with a confused expression. Too late I surmised she was asking me to find the place for her to follow. But no matter; she was reading contentedly anyhow, upside down.

Midway through the sermon Rita's companion had to go "out" and where out was, she did not know. Like a brood-mother, Rita took over; she would show her where "out" was. Again the row of people rose, the two struggled past, and holding her friend's arm Rita, smiling sedately, led her up the center aisle, through the narthex, and out.

Losing his train of thought, the minister paused in the sermon. Was he annoyed? What would he say to this worshiping people? What would I have said were I in his place?

His voice was gentle. "We have some of God's tender ones among us. It is beautiful to see their care for each other." Scanning his sermon notes, he hesitated a moment then quietly added, "God bless them!" And when those ageless ones who knew no yesterdays or tomorrows returned and walked down the center aisle a few minutes later, no one seemed to mind a bit.

That Sunday morning in our pulpit, I saw Christ, the gentle Jesus who rebuked his followers for discouraging the young from coming to him. "Permit the little children to come unto me, and forbid them not; for of such is the kingdom of God." And he hugged them and blessed them, and I am sure there were four-year-olds among them.

Hope B. Friedmann

No Mistakes

My Father's way may twist and turn,
   My heart may throb and ache,
But in my soul I'm glad I know,
   He maketh no mistake.

My cherished plans may go astray,
   My hopes may fade away,
But still I'll trust my Lord to lead
   For He doth know the way.

Tho' night be dark and it may seem
   That day will never break;
I'll pin my faith, my all in Him,
   He maketh no mistake.

There's so much now I cannot see,
   My eyesight's far too dim;
But come what may, I'll simply trust
   And leave it all to Him.

For by and by the mist will lift
   And plain it all He'll make.
Through all the way, tho' dark to me,
   He made not one mistake.

A. M. Overton

The Visitor

For years each day at six a.m.
He went to church and bowed his knee
And meekly prayed, "Dear God, it's Jim."
And when he'd leave we all could see
The Presence came and walked with him.
As Jim grew old the chastening rod
Of years left him so ill and drawn
His path to church is now untrod;
But in his room each day at dawn
He hears a voice, "Dear Jim, it's God!"

Perry Tanksley

Give Me A Drum

Give me a drum to march by
That never misses a beat,
That leads me through the fog of doubt
And fires weary feet.

Offer me faith that laughs at fear
No matter who may scorn
And I will fight the hate of man
Till love itself is born.

Show me a cause that asks for all
The courage I possess
And I will raise my banner high
And stop for nothing less.

Charles A. Waugaman

A Prayer For All

Lord, to this troubled world send peace—
    Remove the hate and greed;
We pray these things of Thee, O God,
    In this our total need.

Impress upon our hearts and minds
    The love of Christ for all;
As down the sinful path we flee,
    Forsaking His clear call.

Reveal thy will for us, O God,
    And make us understand,
And realize our destiny
    Will be as Thou hast planned.

May we forever seek to be
    At peace within this life;
Until we go to live with Thee,
    Leaving this worldly strife.

Clara M. Wenner

The Way To Peace

Is it worthwhile
to pursue a ceaseless chase,
forever driven
as a beast of prey?

This is not following the Shepherd,
but darting ahead of Him.
He promises to lead His flock
beside the still waters.

Drop back, little sheep,
let your life take on dignity
and deeper worth
by falling into step
with the rhythmic movement
of the quiet stars.

Viola Jacobson Berg

The Great Outdoors

From peaks of the highest mountains
To depths of the valley below,
There is life to be lived in the open,
With room for the soul to grow.
From Nature's open windows
Where the earth is always in tune
With the ever-changing seasons,
Man and his soul may commune.

Everett Wentworth Hill

Surpassing Saturation, Lord

I, a lump of clay,
Was once a clod;
Parched,
Until a portion
Of Living Water
Gave me curve and contour
Upon the Potter's wheel.

Would that I might become
Deluged, inundated,
Utterly dissolved
Into a turbulent, muddy
Jordanian River,
Surging to heal;
Overflowing, as God directs,
Across this
Dry and thirsty land.

Celeste Rhea

Beyond The Horizon

Look at the horizon and notice that where the sky meets the water everything seems to come to an end. This optical illusion made our forefathers believe that if you traveled far enough, you would fall off the earth. However, we now know that beyond the horizon there is always more of the same.

In life there is also a point where everything seems to end. Some of us look at that point with great apprehension. However, this illusion has also been out of date since the days of Christ. He revealed that life is eternal. We who believe him know that when we cross the horizon of this earthly life, it is not the end. Saying farewell to those whom we love is a sad experience indeed, but because of the promises of Christ we can rejoice that loved ones continue to live beyond the horizon of our earthly vision.

Robert A. Moore

Passing Melody

I have become
as it were
wind chimes
waiting His breath
to sing
to passers-by
whatever melody
He chooses.

Rachel Rice

"The Lord Bless Thee"

How shall He bless thee?
With the gladness that knoweth no decay,
With riches that cannot pass away,
With the sunshine that makes an endless day;
    Thus may He bless thee!

"And Keep Thee"

How shall He keep thee?
With the all-covering shadow of His wings,
With the strong love that guards from evil things,
With the sure power that safe to glory brings;
    Thus may He keep thee!

Author Unknown

Found

Searching
for something real and lasting,
for someone
who would love me for myself,
as myself, all the time,
I found the One
who had been waiting for me,
longingly,
patiently,
for so many years.
God, I thank You
that You were reaching out for me
long before
I had thought of You.

Dorothy Seaman

The Lowly Eternal

Once more the pageant has been seen.
Once more the miracle has come.

We who donned burlap and gauze
Have worn silk:
We who are penniless
Have given gold.

Mere men,
We have been shepherds and angels,
Prophets and kings:
What is more,
We have mingled as friends.

Is there no end
To what the Child can do?

No end!

Charles A. Waugaman

Jesus And The Children

'Twas in a place where children played
　　The Lord did come that day
But when the children saw the crowds,
　　In fear, they ran away.

But Mothers said, "Oh, we must go
　　To see the Saviour dear;
There'll be no harm or danger there
　　While He is standing near."

They took the children back again,
　　But, Oh, the crowds were thick;
They thronged about the Son of God,
　　Blind, crippled, maimed, and sick.

And as they pushed toward the front,
　　They heard His followers say,
"The Lord is busy with grown-ups;
　　Take these little ones away."

But Jesus heard them and He said,
　　"No, bring the children here;
Of them the Father's kingdom is;
　　To Him, they're very dear."

And when they brought them to Him,
　　He blessed them, one and all;
And so He'll do for every child
　　Who will upon Him call.

He wants their lives to fruitful be;
　　He wants them saved from sin;
So, children, come with open hearts;
　　The Lord will let you in.

Beulah H. Ragland

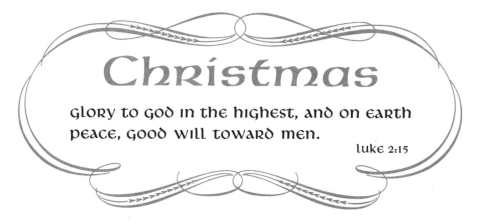

Christmas

GLORY TO GOD IN THE HIGHEST, AND ON EARTH
PEACE, GOOD WILL TOWARD MEN.

LUKE 2:15

What Is Christmas?

Is it holly wreaths and pretty bells,
And softly glowing candle lights—
Or the carols sweet we love so well
Wafting out upon a starlit night?
Is it gaily lighted, traveled streets
In Christmas patterns here and there—
Or that kindly smile from those we meet
Since Christmas-time is in the air?

Is it the fresh and lovely scented pine
With boughs bedecked and spark'ling gay—
Or the gifts to your dear ones and mine
That add the thrills to Christmas Day?
Is it a fireside scene—with love light aglow
Within the walls of "Home Sweet Home"—
Or the prayerful greetings from those we know
That last when Christmas-time is done?

Is it the bounding joy of children dear
Beholding gifts with great surprise—
Or memories fond of the "sleigh-ride" years
Reflected in the mellowed eyes?
Is it the tow'ring steeples of cathedrals high
Where carillon tones augment the "Christmas scene"—
Or the worshipful sounds in a chapel nearby
That cause us to think of "God's Gift Supreme"?

These beautiful things we share year after year
Because of "The Christ of Christmas"!

Helen Donaldson

Christmas

O Christmas, merry Christmas!
  Is it really come again?
With its memories and greetings,
  With its joy and with its pain.
There's a minor in the carol
  And a shadow in the light.
And a spray of cypress twining
  With the holly wreath tonight.
And the hush is never broken
  By laughter, light and low,
As we listen in the starlight
  To the "bells across the snow."

O Christmas, merry Christmas!
  'Tis not so very long
Since other voices blended
  With the carol and the song!
If we could but hear them singing
  As they are singing now,
If we could but see the radiance
  Of the crown on each dear brow,
There would be no sighs to smother,
  No hidden tear to flow,
As we listen in the starlight
  To the "bells across the snow."

O Christmas, merry Christmas!
  This never more can be
We cannot bring again the days
  Of our unshadowed glee.
But Christmas, happy Christmas,
  Sweet herald of goodwill.
With holy songs of glory
  Bring holy gladness still.
For peace and hope may brighten
  And patient love may glow,
As we listen in the starlight
  To the "bells across the snow."

Frances Ridley Havergal

The Wise Men

Seeing that star,
The Wise Men, swift
To bow to the Boy,
Gave Him their gift.

Their gift was gold,
And the bent knee,
Hard metal and
Humility.

Now He, the son
Of Joseph's wife,
Gives then *His* gift:
Immortal life.

This is the hope
Of a world gone wild:
When proud men kneel
To a little Child.

Paul Engle

Merry Christmas!

I wish there were some new way to say "Merry Christmas." Twice today I have overheard that remark. And each time I have said reverently to myself, "Thank God, there isn't" :: The spirit of Christmas is as simple as the heart of a child. It needs no new slogan, and no new sales effort. No advertising agent can lend new glamor to its ancient magic. It is as elemental as the sun and the wind and the rain, as the stars that glowed on Galilee on the Holy Night, and now shed their light on an older and perhaps wiser world :: No, there is no new way to say "Merry Christmas." The tree you bedeck is the same as all the trees of its kind that have stood on all the hills since the world was young. The joy in a child's eyes on Christmas morning is the joy that has filled the eyes of children since the first Christmas. Back of the gifts and the gaiety is an immemorial spirit of goodwill to men :: Christmas is still Christmas. In a world awry with change, let us give thanks for one precious permanency! Christmas always!

Merle Crowell

Christmas In The Valley

Christmas in our valley is a very special day. The people in our valley work hard during the year, but when Christmas is in the air, when the whole valley is sweet with the sound of festive laughter and occasional sleigh bells, and the smell of baking bread, roasting hams and turkeys and cooking mincemeat is in the air, we have a period of relaxation. We make a truce with time.

Speaking of the smell of Christmas, I remember an evening when, with a group of holiday-minded people, I went to a small restaurant on a side street in New York City for dinner. As we sat at a round table waiting for our food to be served, I listened with rapt attention to a man with a shock of white hair, who was drawing magnificent music from the soul of a battered upright piano.

For the most part this elderly man played Christmas music, ranging all the way from "Jingle Bells" to "Silent Night." As he paused between numbers, I beckoned to the proprietor of the restaurant and asked if I'd be out of order if I gave the pianist a small token of my appreciation, and the proprietor smiled and nodded.

So I left our table and crossed the room to the place where the battered piano stood, and pressed a bill into his hand. "I want to thank you for playing so many of my favorites," I said. "You've given me a great deal of pleasure."

He spoke and his voice was as joyous as his music had been. "The pleasure was all mine, ma'am," he said. "I love Christmas and everything about Christmas. Most of all, I love the smell of holly!"

I went back to where my friends were waiting and I must confess that I was puzzled, for holly has no smell! He continued to play old carols and popular hit tunes and the people dining in the restaurant sang along. When our group was leaving, the proprietor came over to say good-by and wish us a Merry Christmas and a Happy New Year. I asked him: "When I talked with the piano player a while back, he said something that confused me. Perhaps you can straighten me out. He said that he loved the smell of holly. Now, hemlock and spruce and pine have a definite scent, but holly hasn't any smell at all."

The proprietor answered: "I guess you didn't realize the truth about Joe. I should have tipped you off. This season of the year he thinks the holly is what he smells, and we haven't told him different. You see, he's blind."

His valley is individual, personal and dark, but he has enlightened it with music and a vivid imagination.

Margaret E. Sangster

Candlelight

I like to put a candle
In the window Christmas night,
That all who pass along the road
May have its steady light
To guide them for a little way,
To send them ruddy cheer,
That they who walk a path alone
Will know a friend is near.

J. Earle Nycoff

Beautiful Things

In winter, I see such beautiful things—
Christmas trees and angels with wings.
A million glittering lights and holly,
Mistletoe and a talking dolly.
Snowflakes, softly falling down,
On our candlelighted town.
My hungry squirrel that comes to eat.
A cardinal, with birdsong sweet —
A barren tree against the sky—
A star, that quivering, hangs near by.
These are a few of the beautiful things
The winter of cold December brings;
And though it's only a flight away,
I wouldn't trade this for a summer day.

Lucille Crumley

Stepping Into The Gift
Of Christmas

Up to the age of nine I spent all my life and every Christmas at Grandma's house. In my tenth year things were different. My mother had married again, and we had moved away. The farm where we lived was only 30 miles from Grandma's, but we had no car.

"No, we can't go to Grandma's this year for Christmas," Mother repeated patiently. "We'll have Christmas here at home."

My new father had to work all day with cattle and pig chores, especially at Christmastide when new little pigs were littering in. Mounds of snow had to be scooped off the open corn piles so that the livestock could be fed. The tank heater had to be stuffed.

Besides, the weather was Iowa-wintry. One blizzard shoved another across the prairie land. Roads were tethered with snow.

The two stoves in the house gobbled wood and coal faster than we could carry it in, but still the cold hung in the air and iced the windows.

Mother busied herself preparing roast chicken and dressing, apple pie and snow white drops of Christmas divinity.

I wasn't interested. I was homesick for Christmas at Grandma's house. She'd be busy with all the exciting Christmas chores that delight a grandchild.

I sat by the window pouting and watched the snow. Fences were cradled in drifts, and I couldn't even see the farm less than half a mile away. Then car lights peered through the snow. A dim, black shape drove into the yard and soon a thundering knock shook the door.

It was Grandpa, thick with coats and scarves, hands half-frozen, cheeks red. Grandma had sent him to get us for Christmas!

My folks could not go. The responsibilities of the farm and the uncertainty of the blizzard and roads, they said. What if they couldn't get home? A sow was making a nest; the stock tanks had to be fired; the cattle bedded; the cow milked and the chickens to tend.

A phone call could have saved Grandpa the trip, but we had none.

I stood in agony during the discussion. Mother looked at me and read the wish in my eyes. "You may go, Tootsie," she said.

Never had the ride been so long, so cold and so happy. Every window in the car was dressed with ice lace. Grandpa had to keep scratching and breath-puffing a spot on the windshield so he could see. Grandpa had bundled me tight in coats and blankets, but still the cold crept into my bones and brittled my toes.

But, finally, I was at Grandma's house! All the cold was forgotten as I rushed up the steps into the kitchen.

Grandma was standing at the stove stirring something. She smiled at me and I smiled back, both of us too full of gladness to do more.

My aunts unwrapped me, and I toasted my feet on the ash box of the big old stove. After awhile my shyness and the strange hurting in my throat eased, and I stepped out into the gift of Christmas.

It was a wonderful day. The nuts and fruit and candy were all just as I remembered and treasured. Grandma and my aunts worked in the kitchen talking and laughing. My little cousins shrieked in a game of hide-and-seek. Grandpa and my uncles sat hugging the stove, stocking-footed, often falling into savory silences.

Then it was dinnertime and the familiar scramble to find enough chairs for two tables full of people, one in the dining room, and the big one in the kitchen too.

Grandma served the food. Lutefisk and lefse to honor our Norwegian heritage, and roast chicken and beef, sage dressing, vegetables and salads and pickles, homemade bread with fresh churned butter and six kinds of jam, pies and donuts and the creamy Kringlas.

And afterwards, the tree. It was set up in the cold room with a Bible under it, a reminder of God's wondrous Gift to all people on a long ago Christmas day.

Grandma had the perfect present for me, a weaving loom and yarn. I loved it! I spent all afternoon making a pot holder, weaving the long slim needle under and over, then over and under, making sure each row was just right. "How pretty," Grandma said when I gave it to her.

The afternoon was finished. The blizzard had stopped and the temperature zeroed down. My throat started to hurt that funny way again when it was time to go. Grandma went into the pantry and didn't come out. Grandpa and my aunts bundled me up.

The snow was crackly and dusted with winking stars when we walked to the car. The starter droned and finally started but then Grandpa backed into a snow drift. My uncles had to come and push us out, their faces red and their breath making white spools of frozen cotton candy in the quiet air.

It was a perfect Christmas—a happy day. I was so glad that Grandma had given it to me!

When I was back home and Grandpa had gone, I showed my gift to Mother. We had supper, finished the chores and went to bed early. I put my loom beside the bed so I could reach out and touch it.

I still have the loom my Grandma gave me. It still works. It is my holiday memory of when I was the most selfish. Because it wasn't until I grew up, married, had children of my own and became involved in all the joy of making a family Christmas, that I realized what a lonely Christmas day I had given my mother and father that year. Then I knew at last, it was Mother who had given me the true meaning of stepping into the gift of Christmas.

VaDonna Jean Leaf

What Can I Wish For You This Christmastime?

Among all the ribbons and tinsel that adorn the gaily wrapped packages beneath your Christmas tree this year, I place two special gifts—gifts that will outlast all others if you take them to your heart and carry them with you always:

One Gift is Joy.

Within this package are memories—memories of special people and special times of the past that awaken almost forgotten Joys, though they be sprinkled with the mellow tears of remembrance. Also in this package I would have you find the Joy of the present—the blessings of daily living and the pleasure of friendship and love. And tucked into the corners are bits of courage and faith in the future, to lift your heart and help you through difficult days.

The Other Gift is Peace.

This one is divided into two parts. One is filled with the Peace that comes to those whose hearts can say at the close of day, "I have done my best." The other part you must share with the world, for to settle with less is to make mockery of the words, "Peace on earth, goodwill to men."

These are my gift-wishes for you this Christmastime—Joy and Peace. Take them, hold them, and may they ever brighten your life with the glow of the Christmas Spirit.

Author Unknown

Christmas was close at hand, in all his bluff and hearty honesty; it was the season of hospitality, merriment, and open-heartedness; the old year was preparing, like an ancient philosopher, to call his friends around him, and amidst the sound of feasting and revelry to pass gently and calmly away. Gay and merry was the time, and gay and merry were at least four of the numerous hearts that were gladdened by its coming.

And numerous indeed are the hearts to which Christmas brings a brief season of happiness and enjoyment. How many families . . . are then reunited.

How many old recollections, and how many dormant sympathies, does Christmas time awaken!

Happy, happy Christmas, that can win us back to the delusions of our childish days that can recall to the old man the pleasures of his youth; that can transport the sailor and the traveller, thousands of miles away, back to his own fireside and his quiet home!

Charles Dickens

Christians Awake, Salute The Happy Morn!

Christians, awake, salute the happy morn
Where on the Savior of the world was born.
Rise to adore the mystery of love
Which hosts of angels chanted from above,
With them the joyful tidings first begun
Of God Incarnate and the Virgin's Son.

Then to the watchful shepherds it was told,
Who heard th' angelic herald's voice, "Behold,
I bring good tidings of a Savior's birth
To you and all the nations upon earth;
This day hath God fulfilled His promised word;
This day is born a Savior, Christ the Lord."

He spake; and straightway the celestial choir
In hymns of joy, unknown before, conspire;
The praises of redeeming love they sang,
And heav'n's whole orb with alleluias rang.
God's highest glory was their anthem still,
Peace upon earth and unto men good will.

To Bethlehem straight th' enlightened shepherds ran
To see the wonder God had wrought for man
And found, with Joseph and the blessed maid,
Her Son, the Savior, in a manger laid;
Then to their flocks, still praising God, return,
And their glad hearts with holy rapture burn.

Oh, may we keep and ponder in our mind
God's wondrous love in saving lost mankind!
Trace we the Babe, who hath retrieved our loss,
From His poor manger to His bitter cross,
Tread in His steps, assisted by His grace,
Till man's first heavenly state again takes place.

Then may we hope, th' angelic hosts among,
To sing, redeemed, a glad triumphal song.
He that was born upon this joyful day
Around us all His glory shall display.
Saved by His love, incessant we shall sing
Eternal praise to heaven's almighty King.

John Byrom, 1749

The Holy Messenger

When God had a message to send down to man,
He, in His wisdom, divined a great Plan;
Not in the rumble of thunder it came,
Not in the skies was it written in flame,
Yet found He a spot that was sacred, apart. . . .
His message He placed within a Babe's Heart.

A mother first heard it that night long ago,
A message of Love that made her heart glow;
It spread its warm beauty from shepherds to kings,
All over the world, down the ages it rings;
That first Holy Messenger from God above
Brought to the world the true meaning of Love!

Dorothy M. Cahoon

Star Light

The stable was lighted by a star
That made dull straw shine gold.
Angel voices woke the sky—
Their song, God's story told.

A baby held in Mary's arms,
Like all small babies are,
Stirred in His sleep and smiled.
His light surpassed the star.

Lucille Crumley

What Christmas Is

Christmas is a lighted tree,
    A candle and a star.
Christmas is a stable where
    The waiting shepherds are.

Christmas is a carol sung
    In frosty winter air,
An angel's wings, a manger bed,
    And God's love cradled there.

Jean Conder Soule

Gifts Of Christmas

May peace be yours at Christmas
The joy of dreams come true,
The sparkle of a winter night
With heaven shining through,
The wonder of believing
A fireside warm and gay,
Contentment rich to fill your mind
This lovely Christmas Day.

May love be yours at Christmas
With candles shining bright,
The frosted panes and star-filled sky
And sleigh bells in the night,
The happiness of going home
Where smiles are met with smiles,
As hearts and minds so quickly span
The intervening miles.

May faith be yours this Christmas
So much your mind would share,
As God and beauty fill your world
Within a Christmas prayer,
The happy sounds—the shining tree
The children's eyes aglow,
The tinsel—wrappings—popcorn balls
And softly falling snow.

A peace—a love—a tender faith
The joy of family dreams,
And then the deeper thoughts and prayers
To know what Christmas means,
A blessing rich to you and yours
All bright with Christmas cheer,
That all the joys this Christmastide
Will last throughout next year.

Garnett Ann Schultz

The Priceless Ingredient

Grandmothers at Christmas, wherever they are,
  Relate to the Day like the Christmas tree star.
Experienced grandmothers, calm under stress,
  Brand-new ones longing to be a success,
Lenient ones driving some mothers to grief,
  Strict ones whose words are frighteningly brief . . .
How could we celebrate without these and their giving
  To Christmas the warmest of loving and living?

Eleanor Alletta Chaffee

Another Christmas

What holy stillness in the night—
What glory from on high!
All earth seems hushed as though to hear
A tiny Baby's cry.

Stark trees keep sentry in the snow
And stars in silence sing,
The sleepy hills in nightcaps white
Brood of their coming King.

No night again shall ever have
A light so like a gem,
No little town shall be so blest
As far off Bethlehem.

No ruler claims the glory of
His humble manger bed,
Nor can he claim for castle high
The star above the shed.

But all who put their trust in Him—
The Christ of Calvary,
May have the love and peace of God
For all eternity!

Esther B. Heins

golden verse

When Christmas passes, as it will,
May gladness linger with you still;
May friends be true the whole year through,
And all things good abide with you.

Author Unknown

The Light That Continueth

Yes, we may take the holly down,
The candles and the tree;
And all the windows in the town
Be as they used to be.
The wreaths may wither and be gone,
The green from streets and marts,
But God grant we may labor on
With glory in our hearts.

Grant there be something in our hearts
To bide there through the year,
When lights are out and all the arts
Of wreath and vine lose cheer.
The tree may wither and be rust,
The tinsel lose its sheen,
These are but dust back into dust,
God grant our hearts keep green.

The carol ringeth out no more,
The bells no longer ring,
No holly wreath upon the door,
No childish voices sing.
But in the hearts of us may stay
The glory and the rhyme
Through all the year and day on day
That was at Christmastime.

James W. Foley

Our Children's Christmas Prayers

Christmas was just three weeks away for our family, living in a little village in Pennsylvania. The year was 1950 and presents had not been bought yet for the children.

We were missionaries and planned to start a church in the area. I had not been able to find a job as a licensed electrician.

The children had asked many times, "What are we going to get for Christmas?" We had never taught our children to believe in the mythical Santa Claus. But, finally, two weeks before Christmas, during our Monday morning devotions, we told each child to pick one gift from the Sears catalogue, and we would ask Jesus for their choice.

We knelt by the kitchen table made from an old barn door. Georgia Mae, three, prayed, "Dear Jesus, please send me a dolly with Aunt Jemima on one end and a princess on the other end, and give the other kids what they ask. Amen." Jonathan (J. P.), five, said, "Dear Jesus, please send me a tinker toy and bless all our family. Amen." Maylou, seven, prayed, "Dear Jesus, thank You for saving us and bringing us to this town. Please send me a dolly bed that rocks. Thank You." Dan, ten, added. "Heavenly Father, thank You for watching over us here. Please send me a train."

Mother Miles asked the Lord for some warm clothes, some warm blankets, ". . . and, dear Lord, give us a real Christmas meal with all the trimmings. Thank You in Jesus' name. Amen." Dad asked for souls. Then little Maylou thanked Jesus for answering all our prayers.

Four days before Christmas the postmistress sent word to come at once and pick up a box which was almost fifty pounds over postal regulations. I borrowed a child's express wagon, hurried to the post office, and brought the big box home. It was too heavy to carry upstairs to our living quarters in the hay mow. We all gathered around to open the mysterious box in the makeshift chapel.

When we opened it, the first thing we discovered was a package of four woolen blankets. Then Georgia Mae spied the convertible doll. Yes, J. P. got his tinker toy; Maylou received her doll cradle; and Dan found his train in the box. My wife, Maylou, had a choice of canned turkey or a baked ham with all the trimmings. There was clothing for all the children and even the shoes fit them perfectly.

A small church in Scranton was God's instrument. They had never met us. They didn't know the number, ages or sizes of our children, but God did. A Bible teacher had asked them to pray for our work. He knew our condition but did not reveal it to them. God laid it on their hearts to make their prayers practical, after our own family had brought our needs before the throne of grace.

God gave us some precious souls, too!

J. William F. Miles

The Legend Of
The Little Donkey

There are many Christmas legends,
And this is one of them,
About the little donkey
Mary rode to Bethlehem!
In his haste to start their journey,
Joseph bought what he could find,
And he led it from the market,
. . . Never knowing it was BLIND!

Now it was a tiny donkey
With a roughened coat of grey,
Blending with the misty morning
As they went upon their way.
And as long as Joseph led it,
It could follow easily,
And thus it was he never guessed
The poor beast couldn't see!

They had traveled all the morning
And the sun had risen high,
And Joseph said that they should rest
Beneath a tree near by.
So he dropped the rope the donkey wore,
And lifted Mary down,
When the little donkey stumbled
On a rock upon the ground.

Continued on page 160

Continued from page 159

He gently took the donkey's rope
And led him 'neath the shade,
Where Mary sat upon a little
Blanket she had made.
She softly whispered to him,
And he seemed to understand,
And he edged a little closer,
And he nibbled at her hand.

And the small one never faltered
Through each long and weary mile,
And Joseph led him carefully,
. . . For Mary was with Child!
And he held his head up proudly,
With frequent joyous sighs,
For his heart saw what he could not,
With his sightless little eyes!

And drawing near the city,
A weary Joseph found
No room except a stable
On the outskirts of the town.
So they shared it with the oxen,
And he made a bed of hay,
So Mary and her new-born Child
Would have a place to lay.

And the little donkey stood against
The old rough stable wall,
Contented just to listen
To the angel songs and all.
When suddenly about him
There appeared a wondrous light,
That fell across his roughened coat
And blazed across the night!

And raising up His Blessed Hand,
The Child smiled tenderly,
And the little donkey staggered back,
. . . Amazed that HE COULD SEE!
There are many Christmas legends,
And this is one of them.
They say it really happened,
. . . Long ago in Bethlehem!

Grace E. Easley

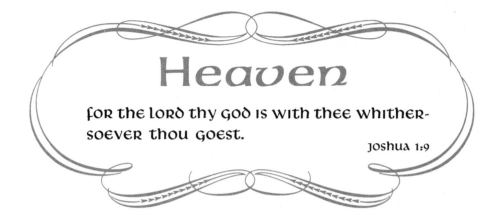

Heaven

FOR THE LORD THY GOD IS WITH THEE WHITHER-
SOEVER THOU GOEST.

JOSHUA 1:9

Solitude

Laugh, and the world laughs with you;
    Weep, and you weep alone,
For the sad old earth must borrow its mirth,
    But has trouble enough of its own.

Sing, and the hills will answer;
    Sigh, it is lost on the air,
The echoes bound to a joyful sound,
    But shrink from voicing care.

Rejoice, and men will seek you;
    Grieve, and they turn and go.
They want full measure of all your pleasure,
    But they do not need your woe.

Feast, and your halls are crowded;
    Fast, and the world goes by.
Succeed and give, and it helps you live,
    But no man can help you die.

There is room in the halls of pleasure
    For a long and lordly train,
But one by one we must all file on
    Through the narrow aisles of Pain.

Ella Wheeler Wilcox

✳✳✳✳✳✳✳✳✳✳✳✳✳✳✳✳✳✳✳✳✳✳✳✳✳✳✳✳✳✳

Just Rehearsing

May it be said of me
When I bow from life's stage,
"He played with all his heart
The role he should have played."
May it be said of me
When life's last curtains fall,
"He played his part with zest
Although his part was small."
And may I hear God say
When from the stage I bow,
"Rehearsal days are done;
Your starring role starts now."

Perry Tanksley

A Sure Foundation

I would not lose the hard things from my life,
   The rocks o'er which I stumbled long ago.
The griefs and fears, the failures and mistakes,
   That tried and tested faith and patience so.

I need them now; they make the deep-laid wall,
   The firm foundation-stones on which I raise—
To mount therein from stair to higher stair—
   The lofty towers of my House of Praise.

Soft was the roadside turf to weary feet,
   And cool the meadows where I fain had trod,
And sweet beneath the trees to lie at rest
   And breathe the incense of the flower-starred sod;

But not on these might I securely build
   Nor sand nor sod withstand the earthquake shock;
I need the rough, hard boulders of the hills,
   To set my house on everlasting rock.

Annie Johnson Flint

GOLDEN THOUGHT

In this sad world of ours, sorrow comes to all; and to the young it comes with bitterest agony, because it takes them unawares. The older have learned to expect it.

Abraham Lincoln

What More Can You Ask?

God's love endureth forever—
What a wonderful thing to know
When the tides of life run against you
And your spirit is downcast and low . . .

God's kindness is ever around you,
Always ready to freely impart
Strength to your faltering spirit,
Cheer to your lonely heart . . .

God's presence is ever beside you,
As near as the reach of your hand,
You have but to tell Him your troubles,
There is nothing He won't understand . . .

And knowing God's love is unfailing,
And His mercy unending and great,
You have but to trust in His promise—
"God comes not too soon nor too late." . . .

So wait with a heart that is patient
For the goodness of God to prevail—
For never do prayers go unanswered,
And His mercy and love never fail.

Helen Steiner Rice

Thank You, Lord

I envy those more skilled than I
In use of words and phrases
To render thanks for gifts received
At divers times and places.
Yet simple words will serve as well
My thinking to reveal;

I know they cannot fail to show
To You the way I feel.
For I am deeply grateful, Lord,
For blessings of a special sort,
That even in the sunset years
Make each new day seem all too short.

Gus Carlson

These Would I Keep

These would I keep: my faith in men,
Though one may stumble now and then;
A faith which helps me still to see
What God intends a man to be.

A cheery heart, in spite of fate;
The strength to work, the patience to wait;
A hand that lifts a brother up
And shares with him the bitter cup.

A spirit calm, despite the storm,
Which sees through clouds, the stalwart form
Of Him who stilled the maddened wave,
Is ever near to help and save.

The optimism childhood had;
The simple trust that made me glad;
The beauty of life in its crimson dawn,
These would I keep as I journey on.

Lida Marie Erwin

Back To School

I've reluctantly signed up for a new course in the school of life. I didn't ask to take the class; I was suddenly pressured into it. What I thought would take a few weeks has turned into a full semester. I've joined a host of others who must study firsthand the problems of prolonged physical pain.

The class sessions are a little irregular. Sometimes class begins at 2 in the morning, calling me sharply and noisily out of a deep sleep. Other times it slowly interrupts a friend's afternoon conversation. But if its hours are irregular, its message is not. Consistent pain takes few recesses.

Today when class was definitely in session I read from Proverbs: "You are a poor specimen if you can't stand the pressure of adversity" (24:10).

I thought, "O, Lord, I don't want to be a poor specimen, but I'm weary and the pressures of pain are so constant."

The course is teaching me that pain is monstrously conceited. Pain stamps its foot and demands all my attention. It's hard to decide if I should have baked or mashed potatoes for dinner because pain holds my mind all wadded up in its tightly closed fist.

Pain also teaches the waiting game. Wait for doctor's appointments. Wait for test results. Wait for the medicine to take effect. Wait to see if a new procedure will correct or change the problem.

Today my teacher gave an exam on patience. I passed—but not because I was smart and had graduated to some upperclassman level of maturity. Rather, because I went back to the text, found the right answer, and wrote it down:

"We are pressed on every side by troubles, but not crushed and broken. We are perplexed because we don't know why things happen as they do, but we don't give up and quit. We are hunted down, but God never abandons us. We get knocked down, but we get up again and keep going" (2 Corinthians 4:8-9).

At this writing I'm still in class. I don't like it, but I know God is in control. I know the truth of hanging on, pressing forward, and running the race. I will not give up or quit. I am God's child, but that does not mean I can skip or cut the classes on pain, so . . .

I thank You, Lord,

For whatever this class will be teaching.

It's interesting to be this old and back in school again.

The semester is long, and I'm tired.

But Your loving arms of strength are longer.

Help me keep that in mind until I graduate.

Joyce Landorf

The Sky

The sky—how far it reaches overhead,
It spreads o'er land and sea.
To know its grandeur I must tread
Horizons unexplored by me.

The dawn brings light to start the day,
To lift the darkness from the skies.
The breaking sun comes through the gray
And brings new beauty to our eyes.

Let morning red announce the rain,
Or fog obscure the rising sun.
What-e'er the weather, count it gain
To make the day its course to run.

The sky gives birth to every hue
That shapes the rainbow through the storm;
In blends of gold, and red and blue,
An arch triumphant comes to form.

The clouds in myriad patterns float
To decorate and beautify.
They send down rain or snow, to coat
The earth, when it is dry.

In rage, it flashes out the din
Of lightning, thunder and the wind,
As if some battle it must win
Before it rests in peace again.

What avenues for birds to fly,
Or jets to leave their haunting streaks.
For kites that strain to soar up high,
Their goal—the heights of mountain peaks.

When day is dying in the west,
Then I must hasten to behold
The things that bring the sky to rest,
Within the darkness—to unfold.

Then sunset spills its deepest red,
The stars, the moon come into view.
They seem to say "God is not dead—
His light is always shining through."

Bert R. Boat

Celestial Cousins

As we ambled along a dusky lane
through a field that glowed with shimmering light,
where thousands of flighty fireflies reign
supreme as the stars in the sky-spread of night,
it was plain that these tiniest twinklers were linked
with celestial cousins at whom they winked.

Katherine Paxson

The Extravagance Of God

Have you ever thought about the extravagance of God?
More sky than man can see
More sea than he can sail
More sun than he can bear to watch
More stars than he can scale
More breath than he can breathe
More yield than he can sow
More grace than he can comprehend
More love than he can know.

Anonymous

The Same Old Sweethearts

"It really seems but yesterday
When we stood side by side,
And heard the pastor speak the words
That gave to me a bride.
Though fifty plus eight years have flown,
How swiftly passed are they;
We're just the same old sweethearts,
As on our wedding day!

"Of course we've had our troubles,
The sweet and bitter cups;
We've had our ups and downs betimes,
But fewer downs than ups;
But through it all you've been the same,
No matter where we've roamed,
In cottage, tent, or bungalow,
Your smile makes home, sweet home.

"Just what the future has in store
Is not for us to know,
The future's veiled to mortal eyes,
No doubt 'tis better so.
But this I know, whate'er betide,
With you safe by my side,
I'll ne'er regret the words that made
You my blushing bride.

"We haven't made a pile of gold
To leave behind some day;
It isn't what we get that counts,
It's what we give away.
We've tried to lay aside a bit
In heaven's bank of love,
And gathered out a few dear friends
We hope to meet above.

"And when we reach the journey's end,
And cross the Jordan's foam,
Behold the land where angels dwell,
That bright eternal home,
I somehow like to think that we
Will both its pleasure share,
For heaven won't seem home to me
Unless you, my sweetheart, are there!"

B. M. Grandy

Waiting For Me

I know somewhere she's waiting,
    As she always waited for
My coming home at evening,
    And she'll meet me at the door.
I will see her smile of welcome,
    Her eyes with love will shine,
I will feel her arms around me
    As I hold her close in mine.
So, why should I be grieving
    As this lonesome world I roam,
I know she's waiting for me
    Somewhere in that other home.

Ken Kelley

❈❈❈❈❈❈❈❈❈❈❈❈❈❈❈❈❈❈❈❈❈❈❈❈❈❈❈❈❈❈

Fallen Leaves

The autumn leaves have fallen and the lonely trees stand bare.
The sky is gray and leaden, it reflects my heart's despair.
For my life's own leaves have fallen, where once were bright and green,
Now lie in quiet stillness, the closing of a dream.

We walked these paths together with flowers on the ground,
We saw the buds, the bluebirds and heard life's happy sound.
We felt our branches strengthen with vitality and life.
The world was bright and lovely with you here as my wife.

Now comes the cold November chill that takes away the cheer,
And all that's left is "Fallen Leaves" and memories of you, my dear.
But fallen leaves are not in vain, they nourish roots and soil.
My "Fallen Leaves" in God's own way, will strengthen my lonely soul.

Stanley Allaback

❈❈❈❈❈❈❈❈❈❈❈❈❈❈❈❈❈❈❈❈❈❈❈❈❈❈❈❈❈❈

GOLDEN THOUGHT

Death is more the beginning of victory than the triumph of tragedy.

Charles H. Brent

Together In God

One you love has gone away, saddest yet happiest day,
Tears of grief bedim your eyes,
  Begun is life in Paradise,
Bereft, you feel you lost your all,
  They've just answered heaven's call;
You walk with God beneath the dome of heaven,
  They are now at home,
Each of you behold God's face in separate worlds of time and space.
So be content though grief you bear,
  Each child of God is in His care,
    While you are here and they above,
      All are living in His love.

A part of me was lost today because a loved one went away,
In sadness we were forced to part,
  An empty ache is in my heart.
Thoughts rush in—tears fill my eyes,
  Great clouds now dim my sunny skies,
And loneliness is mine to know
  As on the way through life I go.

And yet, and yet the memory of all that was is still with me,
Things and places where we two found such pleasant things to do.
So at last I've come to see
  Parting's something meant to be
And beauty shared does not take wing
  It's there for the remembering.

Edith Shubert

Lean Hard

Leaning on the arm of Jesus,
  Walking by His side,
You may trust His every promise,
  He will be your guide.
He has light to gild the pathway,
  Strength to hold you true,
And forgiveness for transgression,
  Grace to bear you through.

He has peace to rest your spirit
  When fierce trials roll,
With His comfort He can soften
  Sorrows of the soul.
He lends hope beyond the shadows,
  Makes the spirit free;
Darkness cannot hide the mercy
  He would offer thee.

He has planned to lift the burden,
  Pressing hard today;
Planned, when earthly toils are over,
  To wipe all tears away.
Reach out, then, and touch His garment
  While He passes by;
Till He comes the promise lingers—
  "I will guide thee with Mine eye."

Fear not, then, to trust the Saviour,
  Trust Him day by day,
Trust Him till earth's dimming shadows
  All have passed away.

Robert Hare

GOLDEN VERSE

For age is opportunity no less
Than youth itself, though in another dress,
And as the evening twilight fades away,
The sky is filled with stars, invisible by day.

Henry Wadsworth Longfellow

GOLdEN NUGGET

Don't keep the alabaster boxes of your love and tenderness sealed up until your friends are dead. Fill their lives with sweetness. Speak approving, cheerful words while their ears can hear them, while their hearts can be thrilled and made happier by them.

George W. Childs

The Secret Of Success

If I could give you information of my life, it would be to show how a woman of very ordinary ability has been led by God in strange and unaccustomed paths to do in His service what He has done in her. And if I could tell you all, you would see how God has done all and I nothing. I have worked hard, very hard, that is all; and I have never refused God anything.

Florence Nightingale

The Way

A little girl was lost in a big city. A passer-by asked her where she lived. She told him the street and house number. So he proceeded to tell her to go four blocks ahead, then turn right two blocks, left half a block, cross the street, etc., etc.

By the time he got through she had forgotten the beginning and cried as hard as ever. Just then a gentleman came along and learned her plight and said, "Give me your hand, my dear; I live close by your home and will take you there." The first man was a way-shower; the other man was the WAY. All her anxiety was gone. She did not have to remember the maze of directions. She simply put her hand in that of her guide and was brought home. So Jesus is the Way. Trust Him as your Saviour. He will guide you through life and bring you safely to Heaven.

Author Unknown

The Poet Of Galilee

Soft words like music Jesus spoke—
Beautiful words so tenderly.
The people thronged to hear His voice
Upon the hills and by the sea.

"Behold, a sower went forth to sow . . ."
He spoke in simple words like these,
And of the grass that clothed the fields,
And nesting birds in flowering trees.

He told about a foolish man
Who built his home upon the sand,
And of its fall when strong winds blew
And floods descended on the land.

"Your Father sendeth rain", He said,
"Upon the unjust and the just",
And, "Lay not treasures upon earth
Where they corrupt with moth and rust".

He brought the people comfort, too,
By telling of God's loving care
And His concern for all their needs,
And Heaven's joys for them to share.

His poetry endures today,
Although it has no form or rhyme,
And every word that Jesus spoke
Will last until the end of time.

William Arnette Wofford

ACKNOWLEDGMENTS continued from page IV

DOUBLEDAY & COMPANY, INC. for "Going on Fifteen" by Helen Lowrie Marshall. From *Close To The Heart*, Copyright © 1958 by Helen Lowrie Marshall. Also, for "Time" by Erma Bombeck, Copyright © 1973 by Field Enterprises, Inc. From the book *I Lost Everything In The Post-Natal Depression*. Reprinted by permission of Doubleday & Company, Inc.

THE EVANGELICAL BEACON for excerpts from "Life Without Mother" by A. M. Overton. Reprinted by permission, *Evangelical Beacon*, magazine of the Evangelical Free Church of America.

BERNARD GEIS ASSOCIATES for excerpts from *The Secret World of Kids* by Art Linkletter with the permission of Bernard Geis Associates, Inc., publisher. Copyright © 1959 by Art Linkletter.

THE GOOD NEWS BROADCASTING ASSOCIATION, INC. for "The Easter Dress" by C. Ellen Watts. Reprinted by permission from the *Young Ambassador*, Copyright © 1974 by The Good News Broadcasting Association, Inc.

GUIDEPOSTS for "Thin Ice" by William G. Benkelman. Reprinted by permission from *Guideposts Magazine*, Copyright © 1976 by Guideposts Associates, Inc., Carmel, New York, 10512.

HARCOURT BRACE JOVANOVICH, INC. for material condensed from "The Old Soldier" from *Four Square* by Dorothy Canfield, Copyright © 1949, by Dorothy Canfield Fisher. Reprinted by permission of Harcourt Brace Jovanovich, Inc.

JUDD & DETWEILER INC. for Selection by George W. Childs from *The Little Gazette* published by Judd & Detweiler Inc.

LOIZEAUX BROTHERS, INC. for "Christmas" by Frances Ridley Havergal from *Opened Treasures*.

MOODY BIBLE INSTITUTE for "Our Children's Christmas Prayers" by J. William F. Miles. Reprinted by permission from December issue of *Moody Monthly*. Copyright © 1969, Moody Bible Institute of Chicago.

FRED B. PALMER for "Thanksgiving Prayers," Pomona, California.

PENTECOSTAL EVANGEL for "My Sevenfold Faith" by Alvy E. Ford. Reprinted by permission from the *Pentecostal Evangel*. Copyright © 1975 by the General Council of the Assemblies of God.

READER'S DIGEST ASSN., INC. for "Rescue in The Gorge" by Joseph P. Blank reprinted with permission from the March 1974 *Reader's Digest*, Copyright © 1974 by The Reader's Digest Assn., Inc.

HENRY REGNERY COMPANY for "Friends Old and New" by Edgar A. Guest reprinted from *Collected Verse of Edgar A. Guest*, published by Reilly & Lee, Chicago. Copyright © 1934 by the Reilly & Lee Company.

THE SATURDAY EVENING POST for "This Morning" by Georgie Starbuck. Reprinted with permission from *The Saturday Evening Post*, Copyright © 1959, The Curtis Publishing Company.

THE UNITED METHODIST PUBLISHING HOUSE for "Reach to the Rose," by Ralph W. Seager. Reprinted from *United Methodist Today*, June 1975, Copyright © 1975 by the United Methodist Publishing House. Also, for "The Last Haircut," by Cholm G. Houghton. Reprinted from *United Methodist Today*, September 1974, Copyright © 1974 by the United Methodist Publishing House.

WESTMINSTER PRESS for quote by Charles H. Brent from *Twentieth-Century Spiritual Letters* by John B. Coburn. Copyright © MCMLXVII, The Westminster Press. Used by permission.

WE ALSO WISH TO THANK

the following contributors and sources for their permission to reprint selections in this book:

A.D. MAGAZINE, Elizabeth M. Adams, Velta Myrle Allen, Ann L. Bangham, Lucy L. Beemer, Viola J. Berg, Bert R. Boat, Sylvia Schooler Brandt, Martin Buxbaum, Dorothy M. Cahoon, Leota Campbell, Gus Carlson, Eleanor A. Chaffee, CHRISTIAN HERALD, CHRISTIAN HERITAGE, Florence H. Cottrill, Lucille Crumley, CRUSADER, Lois Mae Cuhel, John F. Cunningham, Eleanor Di Giulio, Helen R. Donaldson, Nelia M. Dosser, Ann H. Downs, John M. Drescher, Grace Easley, Paul Engle, Dee Gaskins, Lydia B. Goforth, Helen Heberer, Esther B. Heins, Dorothy R. Howard, Mildred N. Hoyer, Ideals Publishing Corp., Ideas Unlimited, Mildred L. Jarrell, Carolyn Jerauld, Ruby A. Jones, Louise Justice, F. Kenneth Kelley, Rhena S. LaFever, Mrs. Elsie Leslie, Jerry Lipman, Doris Longacre, Sharon B. Miller, Phyllis R. Naylor, Nonee Nolan, Katherine T. Paxson, The Quiet Hour ECHOES, Beulah H. Ragland, Celeste Rhea, Helen Steiner Rice, Rachel Rice, Raymond Henry Schreiner, Garnett Ann Schultz, Dorothy Seaman, Edith Shubert, Jean Conder Soule, SUNSHINE MAGAZINE, Louise Weibert Sutton, Perry Tanksley, Ethel P. Travis, Victor Books, William Arthur Ward, Charles A. Waugaman, Clara M. Wenner, Harriett Whipple, William Arnette Wofford, Miriam Woolfolk, Sophie Wormser, Dorothy E. Zimmerman. Also, Joseph L. Voelker, Illustrator.

WE ALSO WISH TO THANK

those contributors from whom we were unable to obtain a response prior to publication: Gerald C. Barton, Ethel Romig Fuller, Frank W. Rucker, Young Americans Riding Into History, Inc.

Diligent effort has been made to locate and secure permission for the inclusion of all copyrighted material in this book. If any such acknowledgments have been inadvertently omitted, the compilers and publishers would appreciate receiving full information so that proper credit may be given in future editions.

ADDITIONAL ACKNOWLEDGMENTS FROM OUR 10 STAR EDITION

"Let the Stranger Speak" on Page 82 was written by Esther York Burkholder. Copyright © 1945 under the title "Stranger at the Peace Table," the Curtis Publishing Co.

"Great Are the Works of His Hands" on Page 138 was written by Helen R. Donaldson.

"These Things Are Ours" on Page 166 was written by Gwen Frostic.

"Beyond the Sea of Time" on Page 169 was written by Garnett Ann Schultz.